FIND Y
a ~~workbook~~... ~~pla~~

MW01173586

This book will help you find your *tov*.
It is enhanced when paired with coaching,
Learn more or sign up at www.FindYourTOV.com

--FIRST PRESSING --
09.18

I didn't put ink in some places. My hope is you will. Calling a book with intentionally open space a workbook isn't right though. Not all the space needs to be filled, but when they are...work isn't always the best, and definitely not the only, thing to fill every space with.

Tov, in my experience, was stumbled upon not worked at. Along the way, I discovered things that helped people a long time ago. They helped me too, so I'm sharing them.

Some things in this book are going to be hard for you. (Some were for me, too.) Even when it's difficult, work rarely gets the best results, it isn't the right posture. So, this isn't a workbook.

Play (keeping things light, having fun, remembering to smile and even laugh) is generally a more helpful posture. Triple down in this, if you're trying to find something. How many times could you play at something and be better off than working at it? I've found most.

When the word play is combined with book, lightness is lost. A playbook lays out and labels who does what and when. They are helpful to individuals and necessary in organizations especially as they learn to live *tov*, but not before they find it. To be clear, this isn't a playbook.

If you don't live your *tov*, creation is left undone. Living your *tov* is the point. Since you are the only one who can, finding your *tov* is the first step. Through ink or empty space, I hope these pages help...they were designed to.

Be warned, messy precedes masterpiece every time. It's part of the process — part of the fun, when our posture is play. Amazing art starts with sketches...intentionally unfinished,
    unapologetically incomplete,
    admittedly experimental (to some degree)
something captured in one moment, serving as reference for a masterpiece.

Finally, the right word. Sketch doesn't transform when combined with book, this is a sketchbook.

FIND YOUR TOV:
a ~~work~~book... ~~play~~book... SKETCHbook

REV. DR. HENRY JOHN GRAF V

Graf Papers
Columbia, Tenessee

A HOUSE OF GRAF PROJECT
EST 1997

GRAF PAPERS
417 West 7th Street #843
Columbia, Tenessee 38402

www.FindYourTOV.com

WRITTEN by
HENRY J. GRAF V

EDITED by
TRICIA MARIE GRAF

COVER ART by
A. McKENNA

FIND YOUR TOV LOGO and
BROTHER DOG LOGO by
TIM BARON

Proudly Printed in Dyslexie
a dyslexia friendly font
because accessiblitly matters
find out more at www.dyslexiefont.com

ISBN 978-0-9910243-0-8

LIBRARY OF CONGRESS
CONTROL NUMBER
2022917034

to the one who likes when I call her doll
before we knew these words
you saw my tov
❤

Choir was the only thing I did all four years of high school.

I fit in.

It gave me a community, or at least as much of a sense of belonging as a kid can have in high school, but choir wasn't my *tov*.This became apparent when I failed music theory my first semester in college. Since I was a music major, this was a pretty big problem.

Actually, I was a double major, music and theater. I must not have failed my acting class because 10 years and 4 universities later, they let me take Acting II to finish a bachelor's degree.

There was a scene where my blind roommate broke a glass getting something out of the refrigerator in the middle of the night. It woke my character up. The open refrigerator door was the only light source in our little black box theater, which was a pretty cool effect. We were both in pajamas.

If you offered me a million bucks, I couldn't tell you the name of the play, or what the characters were talking about, but I remember the broken glass cut his characters' foot and my character put a band-aid on it as we talked.

On the day of the performance, the other guy wore shoes. He was nervous and forgot to take them off.

I was nervous too. As I said my lines, whatever they were, I put a band-aid right on top of his white leather Nikes.

My director, Larry Life, lost it. That day, I learned about something called, "suspension of disbelief."

People that go to a play, watch a movie or TV show, know it's not real. No one thought his foot was really cut, but they suspend their disbelief

vi

and entered into the story. This is a gift the audience gives. It must not be abused.

When I didn't take his shoe off, and put a band-aid on top of it, they couldn't suspend their disbelief any more. As an actor, I'd broken a sacred trust.

Jesus deals with suspension of disbelief when a dad who has a sick daughter seeks Him out to make her better. As a dad with a sick daughter, we've sought out healers from the best institutions with all kinds of letters after their names. Far too many well meaning, powerful but very scared people say, "trust me," then abuse my suspension of disbelief.

The Dad in Jesus' story owns the tension of both trusting and not trusting at the same time. He is candid about clinging to his disbelief while trying to suspend it. Jesus heals the kid, anyway. He seems OK with the tension.

Maybe this Jesus talk makes it hard for you to suspend disbelief. A lot of my friends are guarded when it comes to Bible stuff. That makes sense to me, I've been on the other side of hurt people using the Bible to hurt people, scared people using Jesus to scare people, and it sucks.

However suspended your disbelief is, I honor it as a sacred gift.

Thank you.

- Henry

TABLE OF CONTENTS

MOVEMENT I
ORIGIN STORY

idea ONE
eaT, eAT, EAT

Growing up, there was always more than enough...especially when it came to food.

Some would say that's a statement of privilege or prosperity. It is, but I've had the same experience in the slums of Haiti and subsidized schools of Africa. These are the places film crews fly because they epitomize poverty.

For us, and them, it was a "use every part of the buffalo" situation. Mom worked as a lunch lady at my school and picked up a night job at the newspaper to make ends meet when my father left. Boiled bones and the throw away ends of veggies simmered into soup. Certainly, that's part of why there was more than enough, stewardship always is, so is sharing, and friends were always welcome at our table.

Why does what I learned from my mom, echo to third world countries where she's never been? Her voice carries, but not that far.

If I'm reading right, the very first thing God says to people is, "Eat, eat, eat." When the Hebrew gets translated into English it reads something like "Of every tree of the garden thou may freely eat (Genesis 2:16)," but a little something is lost in translation.

M-akal, akal, h-kal reads like the broken English of an immigrant Grandmother. The sauce simmers as she is searching for words of welcome; she points to the bread and says,

"eaT, eAT, EAT"

"You are welcome. There is more than enough in this house."

More than enough is where the story starts... with abundance, not scarcity.

When we move too fast, like we often do, we miss things.

Reading Genesis, it's easy to speed past, "freely eat," or "eat, eat, eat," to the next line. Don't worry we'll get to the but in a couple days, but why the hurry?

It's not just reading too fast, our settings got bumped and we focus on the negative.[1]

Nothing to wear has nothing to do with what's in your closet. Accuracy isn't the point when it comes to abundance or scarcity, mindset is.

m-akaL, akAL, h-KAL

is about mindset not munchies. Abundance is about focus, not fact.

Where is your focus? Take a moment and think though your day, where do you know you already have more than enough?

The story we tell ourselves about abundance and scarcity isn't exclusively about us. Our organizations and families are also telling stories about abundance and scarcity. What did yours tell you today?

Find a way to remind yourself to focus on abundance throughout the day (or maybe take all week): set a reminder on your phone, or put a post-it on your bathroom mirror, laptop screen, or steering wheel.

When abundance shows up that's not on your page 3 list, capture it. Go analog and carry a notebook and a pen to jot it down (you'll probably fill page 3 quickly, if you haven't already). Get creative and draw a picture of the abundance you see. Take advantage of your phone and snap a picture, text yourself, or record a voice memo. Whatever you do, capture the "more than enough" moments and cultivate an abundance mindset.

SPOILER ALERT: You don't just have more than enough, you already are more than enough.

idea TWO
X

My hands weren't calloused. They still aren't, not like my dad's.

Even his soap testified to toughness. It was called Lava because it had chunks of pumice (about the grit of rough sandpaper) mixed in it. Dad needed something to get the grease off his hands, but deep in the callouses never got "clean."

Len Sweet says some words are so greasy and slimy you can't use them and not expect to be covered in layers of grime. "Good" is one of those words.

What does "good" mean to you?

Talk to, or text, a few friends and ask them what "good" means to them. Be warned, when religious people think religiously they use the word "good" differently.

Name: _____

[] Religious Person   [] Not a Religious Person
[] Religious Context   [] Not Religious Context

Name: _____

[] Religious Person   [] Not a Religious Person
[] Religious Context   [] Not Religious Context

Name: _____

[] Religious Person   [] Not a Religious Person
[] Religious Context   [] Not Religious Context

Name: _____

[] Religious Person   [] Not a Religious Person
[] Religious Context   [] Not Religious Context

SPOILER ALERT: Even religious people in a religious context don't use "good" the way it's used in the Bible.

DEFINITON ONE: MEDIOCRITY

Good to Great² by Jim Collins is on my must read list. He looks at what companies that went from good to great have in common. A great company is defined as:

> fifteen year cumulative stock returns at or above the general stock market, punctuated by a transition point, then cumulative returns at least three times the market over the next fifteen years.

The good companies are at or above average. It was the same way in grade school. We didn't get A's or F's. Our teacher wrote:

on Sarah's homework, on Jason's, and on mine.

Outside religious thought, good means mediocre, passable, but not the best.

There is nothing wrong with this definition, its just that *tov* doesn't mean mediocre.

DEFINITION TWO: MORALITY

When religious people are thinking religiously, good doesn't mean mediocre, but moral. It's about doing the right thing. Moral words are all over the Bible, *tov* (the word that gets translated as good), just isn't one of them.

Can you imagine God saying, "let there be light" and God seeing the light and saying, "it's passible, not the coolest thing I've seen — no smiley face or thumbs up for me, but I don't want to write 'needs improvement' on my own creation either."

Mediocre doesn't work when it comes to Genesis 1. We've paved and polluted creation and mediocre still doesn't work now. There is no average sunset, or mediocre mountain top... marvelous, even miraculous, but not mediocre.

Morality doesn't work for *tov* either. Is the fruit good because it's organic, or USDA certified? Did the Father pay the Son a fair wage, so the Spirit could put a fair trade sticker on the pears or pomegranates?

And what about the second thing Adam heard? After, "eat, eat, eat," God said Adam wasn't good alone. If this was a moral statement then the narrative has changed. People hadn't sinned, and yet we're not moral (if good is a moral word).

Good is too greasy.

Genesis was written in Hebrew. The word is *tov*. It looks like this: טוב

In pears and pomegranates there are seeds. Genesis 1:11 is only one sentence, but says, "plants have seeds" three times. The very next sentence says the same thing again because *tov* is about multiplication.

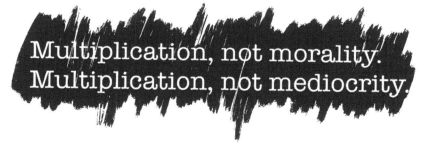

Multiplication, not morality.
Multiplication, not mediocrity.

In every apple there is an orchard. Finding *tov* is all about the seeds. What is longing to multiply in your world?

P.S. The first words people hear are actually, "Eat the Garden Fruit, eat, eat." Multiplication is the reason there is more than enough.

idea 3
ZUCCHINI ARE EVIL

Ryan told me the first dinner in our new house was on him. He's a professional chef, so I knew it would be something special. Listening to Ryan talk about food is magical. Tasting his cooking is other worldly.

My wife (Tricia) and daughters (Kaitlyn and Adeline) have all kinds of dietary restrictions, so Ryan ran ingredients by me. Heavy cream, maple syrup, and applewood smoked belly bacon somehow made ice cream. Smoke, salt, and sweet would play with each other and my tastebuds, he promised. Because of his description, I knew about the meal... then I tasted it.

> # Some things you know, some you know about.

In Hebrew the word for know is *yada*. Eat has always been a *yada* word. You are what you eat after all. Eat healthy, you'll be healthy. Eat junk, you'll feel and look like junk. Either you know food poisoning (and I don't need to say any more) or you know about food poisoning (and words could never adequately express the way even hearing the words "raw oyster" makes your tummy turn.) Once you eat something, you can't uneat it. Your body changes the food and the food changes your body. That's the point of yada.

Hebrew has another word, *d'ath*, for things you know about. My parents and teachers wanted me to *d'ath* all kinds of things from "stranger danger" to **LSD** laced Halloween stickers. They wanted me to *d'ath*, so I wouldn't *yada*.

What, for better or worse, do you *yada*?

I *yada*   TATTOO's (& I have for 20+ years)
_____

(Now it's your turn)

I *yada* _____

_____

I *yada* _____

_____

I *yada* _____

_____

If you're not a fan of staying in the lines, here's some blank space...

12

What, do you *d'ath*?

I *d'ath*   **EDS** (my daughter's genetic disorder)
_____

(Now it's you give it a go)
I *d'ath*
_____

_____

I *d'ath*
_____

_____

I *d'ath*
_____

_____

Here's some more blank space...

In Idea Two: X, we talked about *tov* being multiplication (not morality, not mediocracy, but multiplication). When we let *tov* redefine success, we realize

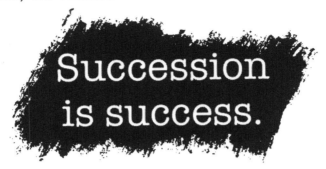

Succession
is success.

In light of that, what do you want those who come after you to *yada*? What do you hope they *d'ath*?

I want my _____ my_____
          (name)   (relationship)

to *yada*_____, _____, and

_____ and to *d'ath* _____,

_____, and _____.

I want my _____ my_____
          (name)   (relationship)

to *yada*_____, _____, and

_____ and to *d'ath* _____,

_____, and _____.

14

I want my _____ my_____
              (name)   (relationship)

to *yada*_____, _____, and

_____ and to *d'ath* _____,

_____, and _____.

Adam *yada tov*, but God gave him a warning,
"don't eat (*yada*) the tree of *d'ath* of *tov* and
evil." In other words, "*tov* and evil" is something
people are supposed to know about (*d'ath*), but
not get mixed up with (*yada*).

Tov is more than enough, but that's not the same
as too much.

Zucchini taught me that lesson.

ATOM Acres is a post-organic farm, at least
that's my description. Ann, Trace, Oliver, and
Matthew (Benjamin, Beatrice, and Margaret help
out too) plant flowers rather than use pesticides
to keep bugs away, and you can taste the
difference.

One afternoon, Matthew helped me start my own
garden. He gave me a tomato starter, and pulled
basil and cilantro seeds from a ziplock bag. Once
you have a plant, you don't have to buy seeds
any more — that's how *tov* works.

We left a spot for Zucchini seeds. Matthew
didn't have those seeds with him. He said to
plant 2, and even made the holes.

I don't have a green thumb like Matthew, but
Zucchini were everywhere. Admittedly, I'd
ignored the garden for a few weeks, but they had
taken over, flowing out of the garden box and
choking out the tomatoes. The basil and cilantro
never stood a chance. When I tried to salvage
something I noticed that the zucchini were even
choking out zucchini.

15

They were *tov*, but like anything *tov* they could become evil... and they did.

Ra is the word that gets translated "evil." It's an Egyptian word Hebrew borrowed. English does this with food all the time. Ravioli, rigatoni, and marinara are Italian, not English. If you've ordered a taco or an enchilada, you've spoken *un poco* Spanish. Chances are good the newly freed Hebrew slaves picked up a little Egyptian along the way — *Ra* was one of those words.

Pharaoh was *tov*.

Yes he was cruel, but cruelty doesn't take away *tov*. There are no two ways about it, his empire multiplied.

Built on the back of the Hebrew slaves, Egypt's power multiplied too. Pharaoh kept the children of Israel from finding and living their *tov*. One way he did this was to claim divinity. He said he was the incarnation of the Sun God Ra.

To be clear, anything *tov* can multiply, so much that it becomes *Ra*, choking out other *tov*. This is what God wanted Adam to know about, so he didn't have to get mixed up in it. We need to remember that still today.

Part of finding *tov* is knowing *Ra*. Where have you experienced *tov* becoming Ra?

I'm amazed how many people carry baggage from learning a very different story about The Tree of Knowledge of Good and Evil. Did you hear a different story?

What did that story teach you about the divine?

Does knowing 3 Hebrew words (*tov, yada, d'ath*) and an Egyptian one (*Ra*) change the narrative for you?

idea 4
ITALIAN FOR ALMOND

Somehow, she knew I was off when I replied, "Fine," to her, "How are you?"

"Effed up, insecure, neurotic and emotional?" Her emphasis was on the "and."

America can get lonely with our scripted response. This was a church lady, her words surprised me. That day, she saw through my, "Fine." She saw me.

South Africa doesn't feel as lonely. When I asked direction, a man took me by the hand and led me to my destination. Part of that may be the Zulu greeting, "Sawubona." It doesn't mean "How are you?" but "I see you."

Think through your day so far (or yesterday if it's early morning) and ask yourself, "Who saw you?" When did you know you were seen?

"Ngikhona" or "Sikhona" are the scripted response, both roughly translate, "I am here." How often do we not show up until someone sees us?

People were made to be known. George Fox, where I had the honor of studying Semiotics, Church, and Culture made it their motto. We weren't made to just be known about (d'ath), but really known (yada). Genesis 2:18 says we aren't tov without it.

If there was any doubt that tov is multiplication not morality, God clears it up telling Adam he isn't tov alone. Actually, this is so early on, he hasn't even been called Adam yet.

As people, we've got all kinds of tov (we will unpack that in the next idea). Biological tov is what Genesis 2:18 is getting at. To paraphrase, rather than translate the Hebrew, "A dude, by himself, can't make a baby."

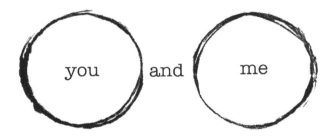

This is pretty basic, but there is also a reason it's made explicit.

Maybe we get it when it comes to procreation, but often we try to live tov by ourselves and it never works.[3]

When it comes to tov the math never quite works out right. Relationally, somehow, 1+1= at least 3.

It's no longer just you and me, but there's an "us" too. The "us" isn't "me," but there is not "us" without "me." You aren't the "us," but there is no "us" without "you" either.

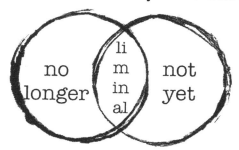

Biologically *tov* is easy to see. The "us" becomes a living breathing person. I met a Rabbi named Allen who put *tov* off a generation. He said, you don't know if you were *tov* until your children have children.

Tov isn't confined to biology, but requires a team. Liz Gilbert writes about authors and inspiration using this language.[4] She'd agree with Rabbi Allen, and talks about her books becoming an "other" and taking on a life of their own.

So who's on your team? Have you caught glimpses of *tov*?

_____ 's *tov* might be
(name)

_____

_____

_____

_____'s *tov* might be
(name)

_____

_____

_____

_____'s *tov* might be
(name)

_____

_____

_____'s *tov* might be
(name)

_____

_____

_____

Legend has it, in the early days, when the Roman Empire was feeding Christians to lions, there was a secret code. If a Christian suspected another of being a Christian they would make an arch in the dirt with their foot. If they were correct, the other would know the code and cross the line with their own arch.

Some call what they drew a Jesus Fish. Fish, ΙΧΘΥΣ in Greek, worked as an acronym: Jesus (ἸΗΣΟῦΣ), Christ (ΧΡΙΣΤΟΣ), God's (ΘΕΟῦ), Son (ΥἱΟΣ), Savior (ΣΩΤΗΡ). The Jesus Fish has been marketed well, especially in bumper stickers, but don't miss the mandorla.

Mandorla is almond in Italian, the overlap of the two circles that creates a third shape. If you visit Rome, you'll see see them on the menu. These early Christians weren't only saying something about Jesus, but about the *tov* that happens when we come together.

When we live *tov* we don't do it alone. Like those ancients, we cross the line.

idea FIVE
oF iTs kiNd

If Albert Einstein said, "Everyone is a genius.
But if you judge a fish by it's ability to climb
a tree, it will live its whole life believing it is
stupid," he wasn't the first.

Back in 1903, "Jungle School Board" was
published. An elephant, kangaroo, and monkey,
had to decide the school curriculum. Each had
a suggestion: climbing trees, jumping, looking
wise, that the other two shot down. In the end,
the three parted ways and decided not to have
school at all.

Long before these fables, along with *tov*, the
concept of *miyn* was introduced. This Hebrew
word gets translated, "of its kind." *Miyn* shows
up 10 times in Genesis 1, but is spelled 4
different ways, highlighting the "of its kind-ness"
even of "of its kind."

Miyn is all about the −ness. Since *miyn* and *tov*
tightly are linked, *tov* is too.

>   the monkey has monkey-ness.
>   the fish, fish−ness,
>   and you, you-ness...

You are uniquely, you. Sadly, if you don't live
your *miyn tov* that part of the universe is left
undone. We are all worse off when that happens.

The elephant and the kangaroo knew tree
climbing was not in their wheelhouse, let alone
their −ness. Often we know what our *miyn tov*
isn't before we know what it is.

Kaitlyn played volleyball in 6th grade. She spent
all season just trying to get her serves over the

net. Finally, in one game, a serve went over. They still lost the point. Her team was so excited they ran to hug her rather than keep playing. "Sports Ball" as Kaitlyn now calls it, is not her —ness.

What are some things, you know are not your —ness?

Keep that list going. If something isn't your *tov*, you have my permission to say, "No." I get it, sometimes we just have to pay the bills, but if there is any way you can stop, please do.

Brené Brown[5] helped me realize fear and shame are often reasons to do things I know aren't my *tov*. When I stop, someone else (whose *tov* it is) picks it up and elevates that thing.

Make no mistake, it takes a lot of bravery to answer this question, but can you think of anything you know isn't your *tov,* but you do it out of necessity, fear, or shame?

Is there a way you can you stop doing it this week, or take it back a few clicks, so you have more time and energy to live your *tov*?

I was awarded a Sabbatical that was scheduled for 2020. Tricia and I had scheduled a week in the British Country side visiting Jane Austen's House and the Bronte Sisters' parsonage. Then, I'd take a class at Cambridge followed by a week in the West End. Our seats for *Hamilton* and *The Cursed Child* were stellar.

We'd fly together to Dublin where we'd part ways. Tricia would fly back and I'd walk the Camino De Santiago, an ancient pilgrimage. Hemingway mentioned it in *The Sun Also Rises*, so I booked a few days in Paris to see where he and Fitzgerald hung out. I had a night booked at Hotel Burguete where Hemingway stayed when he fished and a balcony at the *San Fermin* festival to watch the Running of the Bulls. All this on someone else's dime.

Then **COVID-19** shut the world down.

Since I'd trained to walk 800 kilometers (500 miles), I attempted to pivot and walk the Kentucky Bourbon trail. It was two clicks away from my plan. Three days in, I was picked up and taken to the emergency room because one of those two clicks was water.

Two clicks from *tov* can kill you.

When they tried to rehydrate me, they had to do it very slowly. I guess I was so far gone, going too fast could have killed me.

Some of you know you are two clicks from *tov*. "I'm bored. I can do my job in 15 hours, but they are paying me for 40" is a tell tale sign.

Don't feel bad about this. There's a legend that Picasso was drawing on a bar napkin one day at coffee. He was ready to throw it away and someone asked if they could buy it. When Picasso nodded yes, they reached for their wallet saying, "Name your price."

Without missing a beat he said, "One hundred thousand dollars."

"That took you only 30 seconds," the would be buyer exclaimed. Picasso replied, "You're wrong, it took me 40 years."

Please, don't jump ship. People can get so excited about living *tov* that wisdom is thrown out the window and they rehydrate too quickly. If you must, consider the 25 hours your boss is paying you, a gift to launch you into living your *tov* in a healthy way. This sketchbook is here to help too.

Light is the only time something is called *tov* but not *miyn*.

> God said, "Let there be light."
> God saw the light is *tov*
> God separated the light from the darkness.
> Genesis 1:3–5

This is the first time *tov* shows up in the poem. It is also the way *tov* always comes into existence.

First, someone sees it.
Then, someone says it.
Finally, it's the work of separating
        what it is from what it's not.

See, say, separate, is what the rest of this
sketchbook deals with, but why wait? Maybe
you already see it. What do you think your *miyn
tov* might be?

MOVEMENT II
SUCCESS

idea 1
S-U-CC-E-SS
& SPAGHETTI

Thanks to the cheerleaders at my high school,
I know how to spell success. Seriously, I'm
dyslexic, it helped. Every game was a spelling
tutorial. Unfortunately, defining success is
another issue all together.

I'd love to start today with a story, or a quote,
but nothing fits quite right. So let's cut to the
question; How do you define success?

Living *tov* means succession is success. We'll
unpack that in the final idea of this sketchbook.
We've got some time before we get there. Step
one is owning:

Survival precedes succession.

Wouldn't it be nice if everything was up and to the right,

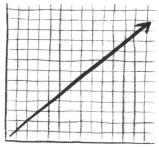

but often the path looks more like this.

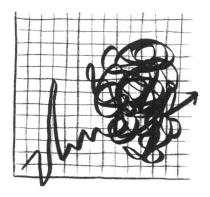

(Can I get an Amen?)

For many, it doesn't get more up and to the right than watching a newborn sleeping peacefully. Brené Brown was brave enough to publicly own both the

> feeling totally engulfed in gratitude, then being ripped out of that joy and gratitude by images of something bad happening to her..[6]

By the time someone becomes a parent, they've experienced enough *Ra* they can't help looking for it out of the corner of their eye. I've been keeping an eye out for *Ra* since the wedgie I got in fifth grade.

When a downward dip happens, we aren't thinking about success, but survival. Us humans are hardwired to survive... even if it kills us.

A long time ago, if a Saber-toothed Tiger growled at my Great-to-the-hundredth-power Grandpa, catecholamine hormones did their job. He didn't think, he reacted. Fight (punch the tiger in the tooth) or flight (run away really fast) were reflexes not options — they still are.

This was good, not *tov*, but good. It kept him alive, and without that he couldn't be *tov*. Without that, I wouldn't be here. I'm grateful for reactions, but long to respond.

Exactly what catecholamine hormones are, or what they do, I don't understand. But, scare me, and I feel them.

In my world, sabertooth tigers are stuffed toys or animated cartoons. We did adopt a seven pound Pomeranian named Coco though. A midnight yap from her (it's not big enough to call a bark) and my fists tighten. I'm ready to fight. I don't know why, but I've never been a flight guy.

Noises aren't the only thing that activate my fight or flight response, boards do too. A few days before a board meeting and those chemicals start to trickle. My board won't hurt me, they're on my team, but something in me wants to survive and thinks I might not.

Everyone has things that activate your fight or flight response, barks and boards are just examples. What is it for you?

Thankfully, my dad taught me to recognize the difference between survival and safety when he said, "It ain't gonna kill you, son."

No one gets out of life alive, but we want it to last as long as possible. Maximizing the chance of survial is what safety is all about.

What helps you feel safe?

Sometimes we feel safe when we really aren't.

There is a difference between BEING safe & FEELING safe.

We think we'll survive when the odds are unlikely. The opposite is true too. Most people don't like thinking about not surviving, so we avoid it.

Getting clear about success is next to impossible if we don't get real about survival first. Money isn't everything, but it's an easy place to start. In *Mind Your Busineess*, Ilana Griffo asks, "What's the minimum amount you need to make each month if you eat spaghetti every day?"

At a buck a pound (which is 8 servings) spaghetti is about survival.

Tricia, Kaitlyn, and Adeline, are gluten free (allergy, not preference). I know first hand spaghetti is a metaphor, but the question still holds. What's it going to take to survive?

Everybody's spaghetti number is different. It will change with age and stage, so revisit your spaghetti number when it does.

Basic things we all need are: shelter, food, water, and rest. What that looks like is different for each of us; So, make the list on the next couple pages your own — add items you need and cross out ones you don't.

Step one is an honest assessment of "what it is." Write down what you pay in rent. If your water bill is included jot a note: "included in rent." If your dad still pays for your cell phone, write that down too.

In the next Movement: **SEE**, we will deep dive into what is, what can be, and what will be, but we had to start with success. Step two, is answering "what it **CAN** be." This is how you find your spaghetti number. Do you need your own apartment? Maybe you do to emotionally survive. Could you have a roommate or two?

When I was in grad school a mug of coffee at Old Crown was $1.23 and refills were free. Old Crown also had free WiFi. They were my office and we didn't have WiFi at home. My combined coffee, internet, and office rental spaghetti number was $37.50 a month. (Thank you Mike and Jennifer!).

36

You may not live on your spaghetti number; That's a choice. The goal is to know it. What is it going to take to survive?

	What is	What will be
Rent/ Mortgage	$_____	$_____
Utilities		
Water	$_____	$_____
Electric	$_____	$_____
Gas	$_____	$_____
Trash	$_____	$_____
Internet	$_____	$_____
Phone	$_____	$_____
Furnishings	$_____	$_____
Insurance	$_____	$_____
Repair/Improve	$_____	$_____
_____	$_____	$_____
_____	$_____	$_____

SHELTER TOTAL $_____

If you've got debt, what is it....

	What is	What will be
_____	$_____	$_____
_____	$_____	$_____
_____	$_____	$_____
_____	$_____	$_____

DEBT TOTAL $_____

	What is	What will be
Groceries	$_____	$_____
Coffee	$_____	$_____

P.S. Nowadays Old Crown ships beans;
you can order online at: www.OldCrown.com

	What is	What will be
Restaurants	$_____	$_____
_____	$_____	$_____
_____	$_____	$_____
_____	$_____	$_____

FOOD TOTAL $_____

	What is	What will be
Car	$_____	$_____
Gas	$_____	$_____
Insurance	$_____	$_____
Maintenance	$_____	$_____
Registration	$_____	$_____
_____	$_____	$_____
_____	$_____	$_____
_____	$_____	$_____

TRANSPORTATION
TOTAL $_____

_____	$_____	$_____
_____	$_____	$_____

_____ TOTAL$_____

	What is	What will be
Insurance	$_____	$_____
Co-pays	$_____	$_____
Gym	$_____	$_____
_____	$_____	$_____
_____	$_____	$_____
_____	$_____	$_____

HEALTH TOTAL $_____

	What is	What will be
_____	$_____	$_____
_____	$_____	$_____
_____	$_____	$_____
_____	$_____	$_____

CLOTHING TOTAL $_____

	What is	What will be
Netflix /Disney+	$_____	$_____
Datenight	$_____	$_____
Vacation	$_____	$_____
_____	$_____	$_____
_____	$_____	$_____

REST TOTAL $_____

	What is	What will be
Local Church	$_____	$_____
Brother Dog	$_____	$_____
_____	$_____	$_____
_____	$_____	$_____
_____	$_____	$_____

CHARITY TOTAL $_____

	What is	What will be
_____	$_____	$_____
_____	$_____	$_____
_____	$_____	$_____
_____	$_____	$_____

_____ TOTAL $_____

	What is	What will be
_____	$_____	$_____
_____	$_____	$_____
_____	$_____	$_____
_____	$_____	$_____
_____	$_____	$_____
_____	$_____	$_____

_____ TOTAL $_____

Now add everythign up,

SHELTER TOTAL $ _____

DEBT TOTAL $ _____

FOOD TOTAL $ _____

TRANSPORTATION TOTAL $ _____

_____**TOTAL** $ _____

HEALTH TOTAL $ _____

CLOTHING TOTAL $ _____

REST TOTAL $ _____

CHARITY TOTAL $ _____

_____**TOTAL** $ _____

_____**TOTAL** $ _____

MY SPAGHETTI NUMBER

$ _____

The "what it will be" column is included because we live in the abundance of a *tov* world. We need to know where our spaghetti number is, but most of the time we aren't living there.

P.S. We won't do it here, but orginizations have spaghetti numbers too. In fact, every departmenat and program does too. Do you know yours?

P.P.S. Survival isn't the goal, success is — real success. Surviving is the first step to success, that's why a spaghetti number is so important, so spend some time on this first idea.

idea 2
FOCUS
UNFOCUS
REFOCUS

Anton went to a performing arts school in NYC.
Being a triple threat (able to act, sing, and
dance) is the brass ring, and Anton grabbed it.
Touring as an *Irish Tenor* and the lead man in
Rent prooved that. Maybe you have a picture of
a "theater guy" in your head. Hold onto that,
but loosely.

Nowadays, Anton owns Blue House Fitness[8]
(www.bluehousefitness.com) in Portland, Oregon,
with his partner Courtney. Crossfit, like theater,
is one of those things people can get overly
focused on, but not Anton. Professionally, he
made the jump from one to the other. Truth
is, he can still do both. Blue House isn't just
a gym (or box as Cross fitters call it) they
partnered with Just Capital Quotient[9] to build a
measurable triple bottom line. For them: social,
financial, and environmental impact matter.

Focus is good, and you'll need it for success.
Fixation is another thing altogether. When we
fixate, *Ra* creeps in.

What do you tend to get too overly focused on, maybe we should even call it fixated, on?

People who have transition from traditional employment to self employment know the spaghetti number is essential, but struggle to set it. I did.

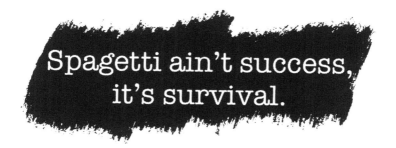

Spagetti ain't success, it's survival.

When Tyler found his *tov*, part of living it was transitioning from security employment at a major bank to starting his own trading / consulting company. He called it a chicken number. "It doesn't have to be filet, but I'm eating chicken," he said.

In a couple ideas, we'll dive into *enough*. It's really not about spaghetti or chicken — steak, saffron ($500 an ounce) or caviar (at just over $8,500 an ounce - White Pearl Albino was the most expensive food in 2021), but boundaries and enough. Remember, *tov* exclaims more than enough.

Finances are easy, that's why we started with them. It's easy to get fixated on them too.

When Adam, the first man in the Bible, was told he's not *tov* alone, God is talking about biological *tov*. It can be just as easy to fixate there too. Abram and Sari, the Grandparents of Israel, did, and ended up using Hagar as a sex slave (can somebody say *Ra*).

Lions are known for getting fixated. When a Lion Tamer walks into the cage they carry a whip and a stool, at least that's what they do in cartoons. Turns out, the stool is much more important than the whip. Unable to focus on all three legs at once, the lion gets confused and stands still.

Like lions, we can't focus on multiple things at the same time. The key is to

not on a million and one things (that's ADD, I know, I struggle with it), but we can't fixate on just one either.

But, on what? To live *tov*, we focus un/re focus on five capitals, but don't fixate on any of them.

When I say, "five capitals," I'm talking about:

#5	FINANCIAL
#4 (maybe 3)	INTELLECTUAL
#3 (maybe 4)	PHYSICAL
#2	RELATIONAL
#1	SPIRITUAL

FINANCIAL CAPITAL isn't the most valuable. On the list of five capitals it comes in last, but it is the easiest.

As a general rule, if you can trade a little cash to get some knowledge, take the trade. You're trading up. It's a good **ROI**. For non-business people that's short for "return on investment." How much money can what you learn from a $15 audio book put in your pocket?

Proverbs is an ancient collection of wise sayings, so this is nothing new.

How have you leveraged financial capital for **INTELLECTUAL CAPITAL?**

On average, a **CEO** reads 60 books a year while the average American reads 12. To make those numbers work, for every **CEO**, 5 people are reading nothing. For every **CEO**, 5 people are intellectually starving.

There are different ways than reading to survive intellectually. *Miyn* is everywhere. Knowing what it takes for you is what's important. What is your intellectual spaghetti number?

When it comes to ROI, intellectual capital will bring you a bigger return than physical. Anyone can tap a pipe with a hammer (physical capital), but a plumber can charge $150 because they know where to tap the pipe (intellectual capital).

Leverageing financial capital for intellectual is another story though. I was a professor at IPFW, an extension campus of Indiana University and Purdue University in Fort Wayne. Students said they were there because Indiana or Purdue were more expensive. Dropping the cash for Harvard or Yale was out of the question.

How much to pay for college is a question most families have. I've never heard the "worth it" conversation in the hospital though. When dad is diagnosed with cancer, no one says, "Chemo is expensive; Dad's life isn't worth it."

Whether it's third or fourth on the list, it only makes sense to invest in PHYSICAL CAPITAL. After all, $10 a month for a gym membership beats $150 for a visit with the doctor, any day. But we all need different things to get, or stay physically healthy. What is your physical spaghetti number?

Here is a secret, few people know. The high tuition at Harvard and Yale isn't leveraging financial capital for intellectual capital, but relational capital. **RELATIONAL CAPITAL** is more valuable than financial, intellectual, or physical capital. After all, "It's not about what you know, but who you know."

Like physical capital, the best **ROI**, when it comes to relational capital is taking care of what you have. How do you stay relationally healthy? What is your relational spaghetti number?

Figuring out a relational spaghetti number is difficult. When a couple come into my office because their marriage is on the rocks, one of the first questions I ask is about date night. Out of hundreds of struggling couples, not one had a regular date night.

Time after time, my recommendation was a date night every week and a business meeting at least once a month. For many, those are the relational spaghetti numbers when it comes to marriage (we'll dive deeper into why, in Movement V: SAY).

Quantifying relational needs is necessary, but feels icky because they are so valuable. It gets even worse when we call the most valuable capital (SPIRITUAL CAPITAL) a capital, but it is and it has, a spaghetti number too.

Jesus started with a forty day spiritual retreat at Wadi Qelt. For him, 40 days of solitude, prayer, and fasting, seems like a ridiculous spaghetti number, but he couldn't survive without it.

8,000–10,000 calories is a ridiculous physical spaghetti (and a bunch of other food) number, but it's what Michael Phelps needed. With 28 total Olympic medals, he's in a three way tie with the countries of India and Columbia. He has more all-time medals than 22 countries. In *Beneath the Surface,* he gives perspective when explaining breakfast:

> Start with three sandwiches of fried eggs, cheese, lettuce, tomato, fried onions and mayonnaise; add one omelette, a bowl of grits and three slices of French toast with powdered sugar; then wash down with three chocolate chip pancakes.[10]

As big as that breakfast is, Phelps didn't fixate on calories. They were a focus. They kept him alive and gave him fuel to swim.

Phelps' breakfast, isn't my breakfast because I'm not training like he did. I don't think I'm ever going to need 40 days of fasting, but then again I'm not going to die for the sins of the world.

Sometime later, Jesus was teaching and healing until after the sun went down. Then next morning Jesus got up early to get alone; this is a bit more like my spiritual spaghetti number. If Jesus, who was God himself, needed a spiritual spaghetti number, I figure I do too.

What is your spiritual spaghetti number?

These spaghetti numbers (spiritual, relational, physical, intellectual, and financial) give us things to

on, helping us to not get fixated.

idea THREE
ENOUGH

"Know when to say when," is a slogan every child of the 80's heard. Skeptics say it was Anheuser-Bush's attempt to get out of hot water with M.A.D.D. (Mother's Against Drunk Driving), but 80 years earlier, "Budweiser means moderation," was a slogan too. It only takes one shift working behind the bar, to see who *yada* these slogans and who *d'ath* them.

Dorthy Parker captured her drink of choice and her limit in this poem:

> I like to have a martini,
> Two at the very most,
> Three I'm under the table,
> Four I'm under the host.

I'm more of a bourbon fan, myself. Mark Twain, who according to William Faulkner was, "the father of American literature," was too.

Remember Twain who was known for satire said,

Too much of anything is bad, but to much whiskey is barely enough.

Wake up with a hangover, or worship at the porcelain altar, and the satire is clear, even if your vision isn't.

Finances are an easy place to define success. When it comes to defining "enough," the clearest example is booze. Each is just the tip of the iceberg. The importance of going a bit deeper can't be overstated.

ălûwǫâh is a vampire-like demon. This ancient Aramaic word would make an amazing name for a metal band. I can see the t-shirt already. The word shows up in Proverbs 30:15, at least her two daughters do, and all they say is "give, give." The next line is four examples of things that are never satisfied.

focus
unfocus
reFOCUS

is one way to avoid getting fixated, moderation is another.

Oscar Wilde reminds us,

> Everything in moderation,
> including moderation.

While we can't unpack everything in these pages, defining enough for each of the five capitals is a great place to start.

FINANCIAL CAPITAL

We've all heard, "Money can't buy you happiness." But that's not exactly true. Up to a certain point ($75,000 a person/year in 2010) the more money people made the higher their emotional well-being (I think that's a technical way of saying happiness) was. At 75K, happiness flat lined.

Having the resources to see your favorite band in concert is amazing. Seeing them once every six months might be cool too, but seeing them in concert every night just gets boring. Enough, helps us not confuse excess with success.

Where is your financial "enough is enough" line?

Years ago I heard about a young professor who drew that line in the sand. When he got married he revisited it, and they revisited again when they had children — spaghetti and enough lines change with age and stage.

Anything he made after his "enough" number was given away. When he had a best-selling book, they didn't fall into the lotto trap. (People who win big in the lotto are worse off financially 3-5 years after winning).

INTELLECTUAL CAPITAL

Bob Goff takes his faith very seriously, but he and his friends don't have Bible Studies. The title of his book says it all. In *Love Does*," he talks about "Bible doings" where he and his friends read the Bible and do what it says

Knowledge puffs up, love builds up.
— I Corinthians 8:1

Shortly after learning how to parse Greek words, a huge intellectual gain, I was in a bible study with a group of pastors. We said, "Enough is enough," We read Ephesians 5:25, and tried a Bob Goff style of Bible Doings.

One guy, bought his wife flowers and cooked dinner before she got home. After dinner, he poured her a glass of wine and instead of asking for sex, did the dishes!

Enough is enough, on intellectual capital is often where a shift from *d'ath* (knowing about) to *yada* (being intimately interwoven with) happens.

A great place to start when it comes to intellectual "enough is enough" is asking where do I know more than I do?

What's your intellectual "enough is enough" line?

PHYSICAL CAPITAL

A5 Kobe, the best beef in the world, isn't about survival, it's about celebration — at least it should be. Four ounces probably isn't enough to fill someone up, but at $30 an ounce, nutrition was never really the point.

Chefs have been fired for stealing Kobe from the kitchen and cooking it at home. Our waitress had never tried it, but somehow she sold my buddy Tim and I on the two ounce upgrade.

Crazy story, but I had been gifted a bunch of money for a dinner, reservations were booked and Tricia had to cancel. To this day, my buddy Tim says it's the best date he's ever been on.

Kobe lived up to the hype, but that extra two ounces was a mistake. It was sliced thin and served on a hot block of pink Himalayan salt. The chef kissed it with a torch. It didn't need anything else.

I savored the first bite, and the second. Four ounces was enough though. Part of it was temperature change, but even amazing things have limits — at least they should.

When it comes to physical capital many of us need to lean to say enough when it comes to what we eat. Another friend, took it too far the other way, lifted so many weights and ate so perfectly that he couldn't wipe his butt. I'm not exaggerating he had so many muscles and so little flexibility he struggled to move.

What is your "enough" when it comes to physical capital?

RELATIONAL CAPITAL

The more valuable the capital, the harder it is to say, "enough." Every teen has felt smothered. Maybe you were, maybe you weren't, but at the time you felt that way.

Early on, Tricia and I learned I need to take trips alone, so that we are relationally healthy. When we were dating, I was playing in a band. My friend Jonathan Rundman played at the same coffee shop my band, *Calling Levi*, did. One of his songs, German Flag,[12] said it best.

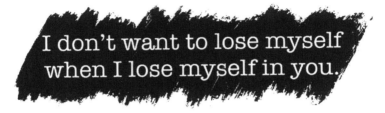

I don't want to lose myself when I lose myself in you.

We'll do a deep dive into this in a couple Movements (Say), but for now, where is your relational "enough is enough" line?

SPIRITUAL CAPITAL

Even when it comes to spiritual capital there needs to be an "enough is enough" line. Peter Rolling tells an apocryphal tale where Roman locals thought it was time for Jewish people to go home after World War II. Since they didn't speak the same language, the head Rabbi and the Pope decided to settle the debate through the ancient language of signs.

On the day of the debate the Rabbi walked into the Vatican and the door closed behind him.

When the Catholics asked what happened, the Pope explained that he'd lifted three fingers, symbolizing the triune God. The Rabbi responded, raising a single finger, not disputing the trinity, but remembering the unity.

The Pope conceded round one, lifted his hand making a circle above his head, arguing that God was transcendent. To this, the Rabbi pointed to the ground, reminding the Pope, God was also present where we are as well.

Finally, the Pope walked to the altar, raised the Eucharist, reminding the Rabbi of the second Adam, the incarnate Christ. As if the Rabbi knew what was coming, he reached into his rucksack, pulled out an apple, and reminded the Pope of the first Adam's sin for whom the promised Messiah must come.

By the Popes account, the Rabbi won, and his people could stay in Rome as long as they wished.

However, when the Rabbi asked what happened he told another tale. Before the debate even began, the Pope raised three fingers and said, "We'll give you three days." The Rabbi replied, "You wait a minute," raising one finger himself.

Without missing a beat, the Pope waived his hand above his head, signaling, "We'll round ya'll up." To this, the Rabbi pointed at the ground signaling "Were staying right here."

"Then," the Rabbi told his followers, "We broke for lunch."

Not only is this the best example for how hard and essential semiotics (the study of signs and symbols) are, it's also a great example of having an "enough" when it comes to spiritual capital.

Oliver Wendel Holmes, Sr. highlighted this when he pointed out

Some people are so heavenly minded they are no earthly good.

So where is your "enough is enough" when it comes to spiritual capital?

idea FOUR
NOT NOW

In 2020, the national obesity rate in America passed 40% for the first time ever. This isn't just overweight, but obese. America isn't the fattest country, in 2021, that was Nauru with 61% of the tiny island country being the opposite of tiny. Still many Americans could lose a pound or two.

One reason obesity has gone up by 26% since 2008, is the microwave. Invented in 1946, it became commonplace in American kitchens by the 70's. The machine isn't to blame as much as the mindset. We want it now.

Writing more and excercising less, put my Body Mass Index or BMI at 29.8. I tend to be a muscular guy, but overweight is overweight and anything above 25 puts an extra strain on your heart.

The scale at my gym measures body fat and I'm at 23%. 50 pounds of me is fat. When I looked at the chart, I was "fair," but 23.5% was close. There, the color changed and "fair" became "poor."

Looking to the far left, for men my age, the word "excellent" was over 8% - 17.4%. That's where I decided that's where I wanted to be.

After a little math, I knew I needed to drop about 25 pounds. It takes 3,100 calories to keep me going at 220. Cut 500 calories a day and I'll lose about a pound a week. If I cut 1,000 calories a day, it'll be 2 pounds. Anything over that, and it's unhealthy for me.

It's Labor Day as I write this, the first week of September. Three months from now, the first week of December, if that is my focus, I'll weigh 208 and be at 18.6% body fat, well within the "good" range. If I keep going by March, 6 months from now, I'll be just under 200 (196 is my goal) and at 13.6% body fat — "excellent." What I want now, will take at least 6 months.

Success is finding the sweet spot between spaghetti number survival and confusing excess with success. Getting there will take time. Dr. Sean Kelly said it well:

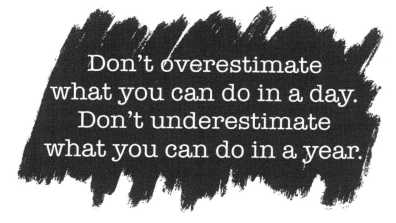

Don't overestimate what you can do in a day. Don't underestimate what you can do in a year.

Where can you be PHYSICALLY in a month?

...in 3-4 months?

65

...one year from today?

FINANCIAL CAPITAL

With a net worth around 200 billion dollars, Jeff Bezos is currently the richest person on earth. He said,

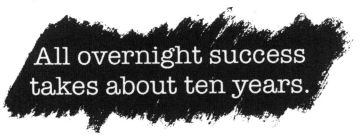

All overnight success takes about ten years.

People forget in 1994, Jeff started Amazon in his garage. Joining the *tres comma* club (currently 2,755 members worldwide) isn't my financial sweet-spot. I'd rather pull a J.K. Rowling and get kicked out for giving too much money away. Even if you are in Biggie's camp,[13] you still need to define a financial sweet spot and a timeline to get there.

Where do you want to be financially in a month?

...in 3-4 months?

...one year from today?

... five years from today?

INTELLECTUAL CAPITAL

Like we talked about on day three of the intro, there is knowing (*yada*) and knowing about (*d'ath*). If your success sweet spot is to be a "world-class expert" it's going to take 10,000 hours.[14]

At an hour a day, five days a week (because people need Sabbath — we'll unpack that in a couple sections), 50 weeks a year (because people either go on vacation, or get sick), you'll log 250 hours a year. At that rate it'll take 40 years.

Doubling down (two hours a day) and your time is cut in half (20 years). When I taught, my boss told me to expect 2-3 hours of study for every hour the students were in class. Since a Bachelors Degree is about 120 credit hours, and a semester is about 15 weeks, students should have logged 7,200 hours to graduate. You can't earn a *Masters* until after that.

This isn't just higher education, Journeymen (electric, pluming and HVAC) all default to right around 10,000 hours.

Where have you already logged a lot of hours? Do the math, how many would you estimate?

Where do you want to add to your intellectual capital?

69

Where do you want to be in 6 months?

... a year?

It takes a season
to grow a pumpkin,
but a lifetime for an acorn
to produce an oak.

... five years?

RELATIONAL CAPITAL

Tricia and I had different thoughts when it came to parenting and responsibility. When I started teaching, I had a student whose mom, although he lived in an apartment with 3 other guys, stopped by each Thursday to pick up his laundry. Sunday, she brought it back along with his groceries for the week.

So, I decided my kindergartener should be an adult.

When Tricia was at work, I had Kaitlyn and Adeline watch me start the washing machine. She seemed like she understood, so I told Kaitlyn her laundry was now her job. I announced this to Tricia when she got home from work and she gave me the you've-got-to-be-joking-but-I-didn't-get-the-joke look.

Later that night, my wife in her wisdom, asked what was really going on. I told her about my student. Tricia reminded me Kaitlyn had a dozen years before college could be a thing. In full disclosure, it turned out to be 11 because Kaitlyn cranked High School out in 3 years, but my expectations were still more than a decade premature.

Sitting on the couch, we made a list of all the capitals we wanted Kaitlyn to have when she left our house. Things like knowing how to set a budget, cook meals, and doing laundry made the list, but our list was so much longer. It included things like how to stand her ground when she was right, and say, "I'm wrong," when she wasn't.

Until she was tall enough to put laundry into the washer herself, it was unrealistic to expect her to do it — so that got put off to Jr. High.

After earning her drivers license, she asked what her curfew was. Because making good decisions was high on our list, we reverse engineered it.

71

She had to be up for work the next morning, we asked what time. Then, we asked how much sleep she needed to function her best. Since work was at 8, and she wanted 8 hours of sleep and 2 hours to get ready, Kaitlyn said, "I guess I need to be home by 9:30pm, that's my curfew."

As Mom and Dad we never set a curfew. We didn't need to.

Movement V: SAY ends up diving deep into relationships, so for now, just pick one. Relationship timelines are different, with Kaitlyn ours was 11 years. Maybe you need to have a conversation this week. Perhaps letting off the gas and thinking in quarters, years, and decades, is better for you.

Where can my relationship with_____ be
                                (name)
in _____ weeks?
(number)

..... how about in _____ months?
                   (number)

...how about in _____ years?
                (number)

Where can my relationship with_____be
(name)
in _____ weeks?
(number)

..... how about in __ months?
(number)

...how about in _____ years?
(number)

SPIRITUAL CAPITAL

No matter what you think of Jesus, he was a great spiritual leader. His ministry only lasted about 3 years and he spent most of it making disciples. The last thing he told these disciples, was to make disciples.[15] Disciples made disciples, who then made disciples. Although there was brutal persecution, 300 years later Jesus followers made up more than half of the known world and became the religion of the empire.

This timeline is more than anyone's lifetime, and as spiritual capital tends to do, puts things in perspective.

Where do you want your spiritual capital to be in 3 months?

...in a year?

...in 3 years?

idea FIVE
BUS NUMBER

The Church that let me be their Senior Pastor, grew really quickly and took out a half million dollar life insurance policy on me. Since that was the same amount as the annual budget, I was honored. Is that really what I'm worth? Is that what it would take to replace me?

I did the math, and years of watching C.S.I. before bed caught up to me. The church would have a lot left over if I kicked the bucket.

When Keith, one of the elders, asked, "What's your bus number?" It didn't add to my murderous thoughts until he clarified. My blank stare must have given me away. I had no clue what a bus number was.

"How many people could do your job if you got hit by a bus?" He wasn't plotting my murder, but pointing out I had become irreplaceable — and not in a good way.

Goldilocks would say not hitting your spaghetti number is too cold, and not stopping, or doing something different, when you are at enough, is too hot. This is the sweet spot, not success, because bears still come home.

A sweet spot without succession collapses under its own weight. It takes some time, I suggest a

Sabbatical cycle (we'll unpack that a bit in MOVEMENT IV: SABBATH, and do a deep dive in the last Movement: SUCCESSION), but its worth it because

Succession is success.

Finding the sweet spot is "necessary not sufficient."[16]

Whatever you think about Jesus, you can't deny he started a movement. Many, measure time based on him — it's been 2,022 years since he did what he did. One thing Jesus did, that doesn't get unpacked nearly enough, was pay attention to his bus number. He did this from day one (well, day forty-one).

Matthew says, Jesus got baptized and took a forty day sabbatical.[17] After a sermon or two, Jesus started dealing with his bus number.

One of the ways we know *tov* is multiplication not morality is that God told Adam, "dudes by themselves, can't make babies," or to translate Genesis 2:18 more precisely, "'it is *lo tov* for man to be alone." Not *tov*, doesn't quite cut it. Adam lacked the very thing *tov* was – multiplication.

So Jesus doesn't deal with succession through individuals, but pairs. First, he asks Simon and his brother Andrew to follow him. Then, in case anyone missed the call back to *tov*, he asked another set of brothers: James and John.

Being a disciple isn't just about knowing what a teacher knew, but doing what the teacher did.

It was a bus number thing. When Jesus sent his disciples out, to do what he did, he sent them out two-by-two,[18] not individually — because *lo tov*.

Time for some math...

$$12 \div 2 = \rule{3cm}{0.4pt}$$

... and a third grade story problem... If each of these pairs did what Jesus did and gathered up a dozen disciples themselves, how many disciples would there be?

$$\rule{3cm}{0.4pt} \; X \; \rule{3cm}{0.4pt} \; = \; \rule{3cm}{0.4pt}$$

On one page, Jesus is sending out his 12 disciples.[19] Flip the page and he is sending out 72 people.[20] These aren't his disciples, but his grand-disciples. Some Rabbis[21] teach that children aren't *tov*, but grand-children are. The thinking is "great you can multiply, but can they?"

A bit more math, Jesus sent these 72 out two-by-two as well...

$$72 \div 2 = \rule{3cm}{0.4pt}$$

If they did what their teacher did how many great-grand disciples would Jesus have?

$$\rule{3cm}{0.4pt} \; X \; 12 \; = \; \rule{3cm}{0.4pt}$$

If they all got together, like a disciple family reunion, how many disciples would be present?

$$\underline{\hspace{3cm}} + \underline{\hspace{2cm}} + \underline{\hspace{2cm}}$$

original disciples   grand disciples   great grand disciples

$$= \underline{\hspace{4cm}}$$

What do you think the odds are, that when Paul reminds the church in Corinth that Jesus "appeared to more than 500 of the brothers and sisters at the same time"[22] after his resurrection he was making a not-so-subtle point about *tov?*.

Derek Silvers, best known for: [23]

had to quit his job as a librarian at Warner Chappell Music. He figured, "It wasn't my bosses' fault I wanted to quit, so why should I make it his problem?" Before telling his boss he quit, he offered his job, at his salary, to his friend Nicki. Then, he spent a week training her; so, she could do the job because it seemed "respectful and considerate." Silvers was living *tov.*

In a *tov* world (if I've said it once, I've said it three times...once on 14, once on 76, and now)

Succession is success.

Before we can talk about succession, and we will dedicate **MOVEMENT VII** to talkign about succession, let's figure out your *miyn tov*. The good news is, it's three simple steps:

see,   say,   separate.

MOVEMENT III
SEE

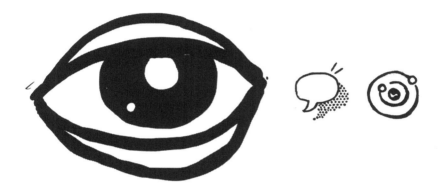

idea ONE
GOD SAW FIRST

Which came first, the chicken or the egg? It's a classic for a reason. This question tells you how people process information and gives you a hint at how they build a case. Also, people tend to get hung up on order.

For Star Wars fans, George Lucas wearing a "Han shot first" t-shirt should have settled the debate. It was his story to tell.

Actors are expensive, so movies are not shot in order. Filmmakers think about the order of the story in preproduction, then play with it in post. Jean-Luc Godard,[24] granddaddy of French New Wave film said,

> A story should have
> a begining, a middle, & an end,
> but not necessarily in that order.

Once you realize a T-shirt tells a story, you know the authors intent — at least when it comes to Star Wars. If you think clothing is just a covering you'll miss the story. Likewise, *tov* gets lost when we forget the Bible starts with a poem.

God said, "Let there be light."
and God saw the light was *tov*
and God separated
    the light from the darkness.
— Genesis 1:3–4

The fact that it's a poem lets us know, God saw
first. Poems, while artistic, can also be accurate.

POETRY ≠ PRETEND

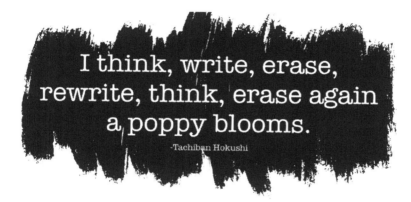

I think, write, erase,
rewrite, think, erase again
a poppy blooms.

-Tachiban Hokushi

Hoskushi's poem is a Haiku.[25] It starts and ends
with a five syllable line, between them is a seven
syllable line — that's it. If it follows those rules
it's a haiku, if it doesn't, it's not. That's what
makes it a poem.

It's also true, ask anyone who has ever made
anything — even George Lucas followed
Hokusai's haiku.

During this project, my days start early. I'm
pastoring a church, so I don't have the luxury of
writing in a secluded cabin like authors in movies.
That wouldn't work for me anyway.

At the end of a day, my brain is mush. When I
first wake up I can hear differently.

How do I say that in a sonnet? Can I communicate in haiku?

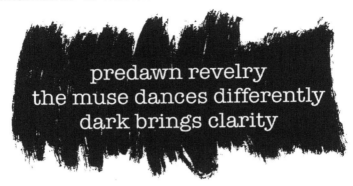

predawn revelry
the muse dances differently
dark brings clarity

My poem had a process. Think, write, erase, rewrite, think, erase again.

> 5-7-5 forces something.
> 5-7-5 makes it a haiku.

Poetry is structure. It doesn't comment on fact or fiction.

It's one thing to know (remember *d'ath*), but another to try (*yada*).

Since this is sketchbook, try your hand at a haiku. Put one syllable on each blank:

_____ _____ _____ _____ _____

_____ _____ _____ _____ _____ _____ _____

_____ _____ _____ _____ _____

5-7-5 makes a haiku. Fourteen lines in iambic pentameter and you've got a sonnet. Like haiku, it's all about the syllables, each line of a sonnet has 10.

Shall I compare you to a summers day?
-William Shakespeare

Sonnets[26] also follow rhyming patters. My favorite to write is the ABBA ABBA meaning lines 1, 4, 5, and 8 all end with a rhyming word (day, may, play, say). Lines 2, 3, 6, and 7 end on a different set of rhyming words, and all eight of these lines ask a question.

Is there a question you are dealing with? Well then, sketch a sonnet.

(A) _____ _____ _____ _____ _____

_____ _____ _____ _____ _____

(B) _____ _____ _____ _____ _____

_____ _____ _____ _____ _____

(B) _____ _____ _____ _____ _____

_____ _____ _____ _____ _____

(A) _____ _____ _____ _____ _____

_____ _____ _____ _____ _____

(A) —— —— —— —— ——

—— —— —— —— ——

(B) —— —— —— —— ——

—— —— —— —— ——

(B) —— —— —— —— ——

—— —— —— —— ——

(A) —— —— —— —— ——

—— —— —— —— ——

After those 8 lines, the next six are **CDE CDE**
or **CDC DCD** and they answer the question.

(C) —— —— —— —— ——

—— —— —— —— ——

(D) —— —— —— —— ——

—— —— —— —— ——

if you pick "**E**" stick to the left (**CDE** comes
next), if "**C**" to the right (**DCD** is the rhyming
pattern).

(E or **C**) —— —— —— —— ——

—— —— —— —— ——

(C or D) _____ _____ _____ _____ _____

_____ _____ _____ _____

(D or C) _____ _____ _____ _____ _____

_____ _____ _____ _____

(E or D) _____ _____ _____ _____ _____

_____ _____ _____ _____

Becoming a poet isn't the point, playing with words is. When we play we see in a new way.

Songs are poems that call us to dance. Maybe that's why the Bible starts with one.

On a technical note, the creation poem starts with a *chiasm*, a poetic feature like the ABBA of sonnets. The Greek letter *chi*, the reason it's called a *chiasm*, looks like this X. Every pirate knows, "X marks the spot."

God said, "Let there be light."

God saw the light was *tov*

God separated the light from the darkness.

X marks *tov.*

X marks see — because see is where *tov* starts.

idea 2
VISION NEEDS VOCAB

Avi, wrote a book for kids on writing called

a beginning,
a muddle,
and an end.

It's next to impossible to find because google assumes a typo and searches for middle not muddle, but I guess that's the point. The middle, is muddled.

When it comes to finding *tov,* see and say are muddled. Even though see comes first, you can't see unless you can say. Vision needs vocabulary.

Tall is small,
Grande means medium, and
Venti equals large.

It's not on the menu, but Short is extra-small. Even though you can only get some iced drinks in it, Trenta (31 ounces) is extra-large.

So why not small, medium, and large? Because Starbucks understands language creates culture.

After growing a church and seeing it decline from a distance, Mike Breen discovered discipleship. Discipleship had been a huge feature of the Bible all along, but for all practical purposes was lost. Realizing the importance of building a discipleship culture, he created Lifeshapes, a discipleship language.[27]

In churches worldwide discipleship became a thing again because language creates culture. As we peel the onion there is a layer beneath that though. It's a bit paradoxical, but we can't see until we have a way to talk about what we see — vision needs vocabulary.

Maybe, just maybe, we need to learn to draw, so we can see. Artists and art teachers agree:

> The magical mystery of drawing ability seems to be, in part at least, an ability to shift the brain state to a different mode of seeing / perceiving. When you see in the special way in which experienced artists see then you can draw.
> — Betty Edwards[28]

Yes, I'm going to ask you to draw...or at least sketch please don't chuck this book across the room. It's supposed to be fun.

Since being an artist, at least drawing, is more about seeing than anything else; Nowadays, when someone says, "I can't draw," what I hear is, "I won't see." Gordon Mackenzie, whose job title at Hallmark was *Creative Paradox* noticed this when he asked who the artists were:

FIRST GRADE
E*n Mass* the children leapt from their chairs, arms waving wildly, eager hands trying to reach the ceiling.
Every Child was an artist.

SECOND GRADE
About half the kids raised their hands, shoulder high no higher. The raised hands were still.

THIRD GRADE
At best, 10 kids out of 30, would raise a hand.
Tentatively. Self-consciously.[29]

We all see the trajectory. Chances are good, you're a few years past third grade and somewhere along the line stopped seeing. This is nothing new. 2,000 years ago when Jesus said, "seeing they do not see, and hearing they do not hear, nor understand,"[30] Jesus was quoting Isaiah who said it more than 700 years before him.

The good news is it's not too late. Vocabulary can still give you vision. Learning to draw will help you to see. Actually, this is great news because see is the first step to finding and living *tov*.

It gets even better, if the word draw freaks you out, steal vocabulary from Sunni Brown who advocated doodling, not drawing. (If you feel a little more comfortable doodling than drawing, you see how language creates culture.)

Sunni and her friend David Grey came up with a "visual alphabet."[31]

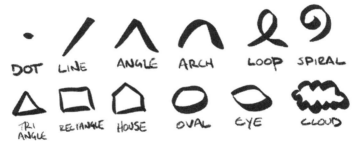

With these 12 "letters" you spell a picture, or draw it, or doodle it — let's give it a try. I'm in a coffee shop as I write this, so I've got a paper cup of coffee: oval, line, line, arch. Give it a try. Sketch one here.

To add the lid, it's: oval, line, line, arch. And that little cardboard thing that keeps me from burning my hand is just two more arches and two more lines (Find some crayons and it gets even more fun).

What's in front of you: a phone, a chair, a table? ... Pick whatever you'd like. What do you see? (Use Sunni's words before you attempt your doodle.)

——————, ——————, ——————, ——————,

——————, ——————, ——————, ——————...

Now go for it!

(Pages like this are intentionally blank for notes
and doodle; fill them up, today and throughout.)

idea THREE
WHAT IS?

Draw or doodle...

    sketch or scribble...

        it's about what you see.

Finding *tov* is no different. Sometimes, I know something is there, but I can't see it. This can be as simple as the fourth leg on a chair. When it comes to drawing, at least in the beginning, if you can't see it, you don't sketch it.

Owning what we really see is the first, and hardest part of capturing it.

They call me Henry. My birth certificate adds John Graf V — that's a Roman numeral 5 at the end.

I've got a diploma with Reverend before my name and by the time you are reading this another that adds Doctor. (Writing this is a final part of that degree.) If you look at my driver's license you'll see I'm male, 6 feet tall, 220 pounds, and born in 1975. As I write this, my zip code is 46835 — Fort Wayne, Indiana. Chances are good, that by the time you are reading this, it'll be 3840-something.

It's hard to see what is. Twice, in that one paragraph, I jumped over what can be to what will be. The fact is, I know the degree and zip code *will be* because I started with seeing *what is*,

    then moved to seeing *what can be*,

    then made the choice of *what will be*,
but that comes later.

We start by seeing what is, and as *the Flash* sings, "it starts with me."[32]

WHAT IS – ME EDITION
(Just The Facts)

They call me _____
                    (name)

My birth certificate says _____ ____ ____
                          (month)   (day) (year)

and a little math will tell you I'm ____ years old.

My driver's license says I'm ____ feet ____ inches

tall, weigh _____ pounds,

and live in _____, ____
             (city)   (state)

You can tell by looking at the picture that I'm

_____.
(ethnicity)

What's missing?

What are other "what is" things that should be
seen?

My dad was a draftsman, at least in his younger years. Drafting ain't doodling. It's a really specific kind of drawing. The goal is to shift perspective and show all the sides. A chair is drawn like this — you can see all the legs, but not all at the same time.

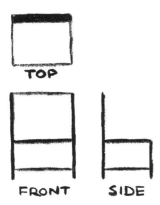

Chances are, "just the facts" didn't paint a great picture of "what is" when it comes to you. You are multifaceted, so let's be draftsmen and change shift angles.

Like I said, draw or doodle, sketch or scribble, it's about what you see. But Haiku is about syllables, not what you see, but what you hear. Sonnet takes hearing to the next level and adds a rhyme scheme. What would happen if you haiku yourself?

___ ___ ___ ___ ___

___ ___ ___ ___ ___ ___

___ ___ ___ ___ ___

Like the number of syllables in a haiku (5–7–5), people pay attention to numbers in Hebrew poems too.

Genesis starts with seven Hebrew words (This is what it looks like in Hebrew)

בראשית ברא אלהים את השמים ואת הארץ:

In the beginning (בראשית) God (אלהים) created (ברא) the (את) heavens (השמים) and the (ואת) earth (הארץ).

The very next line of the poem tells what is.

והארץ היתה תהו ובהו וחשך על-פני תהום ורוח אלהים מרהפת על-פני המים:

And the earth (והארץ) was (היתה) formless (תהו) and void (ובהו) And darkness (וחשך) was upon (על) the face (פני) of the deep (תהום) and the spirit (ורוח) of God (אלהים) moved (מרהפת) upon (על) the face (פני) of the water (המים)

Seeing the earth was formless and empty, was the first step to giving it form and filling it up. What can be, is always based on what is. There are seven days of creation.

The poem starts with seven words in the first line. Since the poem, and all creation is about *tov*, the word count of the second line multiplies the first (it's 14 words) to tell the story.

Sometimes seing what is, means answering questions, sometimes it takes drawing (or drafting it out), other times poetry is the clearest way to see. When it comes to seeing you, a self portrait might tell you more about "what is" than words can. You've got the space.

People that say, "I can't draw," often end up with drawings that tell a story of what is. So give it a try — you've got the basic doodling vocabulary.

idea 4
EYES & EARS OF FAITH

One time being in the dark was enough for me.

We were in Southern Indiana when Dad took us spelunking (that's the fancy way to say crawling around in caves). After squiggling and squirming for some time we were deep in the earth and my brother suggested we turn off our headlamps.

It was dark.

Not dim, the thing we usually call dark, but dark. Nobody could see anything. I flicked my fingers so close to my face I could hear them. I even bumped my nose a time or two. Trying to see something, I flapped my wrist, and felt wind, but still saw nothing because, it was dark.

You can't see in the dark, at least not if you're seeing with eyes.

Faith, at least the way the Bible uses it, isn't a uniquely religious word. Hebrews 11:1 says, it's the "substance / confidence / assurance" (the word is ὙΠόστασις and it only shows up in the New Testament five times, so it's tough to translate) "of things hoped for." Then it gets poetic, the author flips it and says the same things a different way (it's called a parallelism). Faith is "certainty / assurance / conviction (ἔλεγχος is only used one other time, in 2 Timothy 3:16) of things we don't see."

When a parent holds a newborn they use words like beautiful, even though the child is red and blotchy, covered in goo, and has a misshapen head. Parents see with eyes of faith.

A coach who calls a kid "champ," even though they trip over the soccer ball more often than they kick it, does the same. Coaches say, "That kid has promise." A theusaurus reminds us "promise" is synonomous with "faith." Those coaches see what's not there, at least not yet.

God saw the light, before God separated it from the darkness. When God saw first, God saw with faith.

Spolier alert: When you are living your *tov* and helping others to do likewise you'll be seen as a leader.

Leadership, like zucchini is supercharged with *tov*. Sadly, leaders can, and often do, become *Ra*. That's why, when a friend is appointed to a leadership position I gift, *Summoned to Lead* and a bottle of Shackleton.[33]

Dr. Sweet challenged the metaphor, arguing:

> What matters most is not the clarity of your eyes, but the charity of your heart and the clearness of your ears.

It's as if he would see my see example, and raise with two hear examples. Still,

> the phenomenon of leadership always will remain misty — and always should. But failure to probe the currency of hearing as well as the currency of seeing is one reason why leadership remains one of the most studied and least understood phenomenon of the last century.[34]

When Samuel was summoned[35] it was through a voice not a vision.
Hearing not seeing.
The ear not the eye.

101

Samuel thought it was his friend and mentor Eli, so he ran to him, but Eli didn't hear the voice. Like God, parents and coaches see with eyes of faith; Samuel heard with ears of faith.

Faith is mushy. Because all metaphors, highlight and hide[36] it's never really been about seeing or hearing. Even Betty Edwards[37] when talking about drawing used a slash after see. Remember:

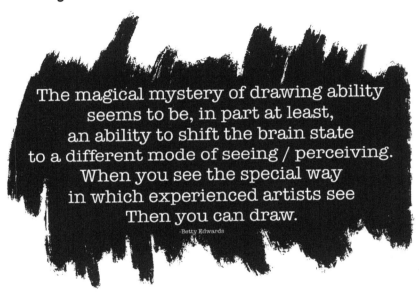

The magical mystery of drawing ability
seems to be, in part at least,
an ability to shift the brain state
to a different mode of seeing / perceiving.
When you see the special way
in which experienced artists see
Then you can draw.
-Betty Edwards

Maybe "sense" is a more accurate word. (Yes, you read that quote back on page 89 too.) So let's play with that. Here are some things have helped me,

SEE WITH EYES

1. Draw, learning to draw, and talking to drawers.

2. Shoot, learning to shoot, and talking to photographers (and filmmakers).

3. Looking at art, and making friends with gallery owners.

What has helped you see?

Every now and again former Disney Imagineer, Joe Rohde,shares art history songs on Instagram (@joerohde). The images are collected from an artist / genre. He then rewrites the lyrics of a pop song and they serve as the caption.

Technically, eyes pick up electromagnetic radiation, maybe I'll play with this on my Instagram as I explore color. For me, the song would be *Good Vibrations* by The Beach Boys.[38] Vibrations are what our next sense, hearing, picks up.

HEARING WITH EARS

The top three things that helped me hear are:

1. Poetry & Poets, the two are inseparable to me. For years, Wednesday nights were dedicated to a writers group at Old Crown. The group was lucky enough to have two poets: Lauren[39] and Sophia.[40]

2. Music — I've made friends with musicians from producers to players.

3. Therapy — My counselors have always practiced and taught reflective listening.

If you are trying to learn to listen, with ears or with faith give 'em a go. Then again maybe you have things that have helped you here... What are they?

TASTING WITH NOSE

My final semester of college was easy: Tennis, Ceramics for non-majors, Acting II (I'd taken Acting I a decade earlier), and HTM 491.
The Hotel, Tourism, and Management (HTM) department called 491 Beverage Management, but we called it wine tasting. Before I'd heard the word mandorla, in that class, I learned the nose and mouth are connected.

A couple things that helped me smell were:

1. Lighting a candle — I've got scents for every season.

2. Making friends with a perfumer. (JP from HYDE + ALCHEMY put together a "discovery kit" check it out at www.HydeAlchemy.com)

What are some things that have helped you smell better? (No pun intended.)

Other than smelling, when it comes to taste, two things have changed my world:

1. Learning to cook.

2. Eating with a chef. (Keep an eye open for "chef dinners" — the best ones are at farms.)

105

What has helped you taste, not just eat?

FEELING WITH...

Taste and smell get a little mandorlic, but feeling is mushy. Are we talking about feeling with our hands, or our heart?

We like the idea of 5 senses. They are easy to teach kids: eyes see, ears hear, nose smells, mouth tastes, and skin feels. Doodling a cat makes it even easier because with them whiskers feel and whiskers are easier to draw than hands. Five[41] is a good place to start, but

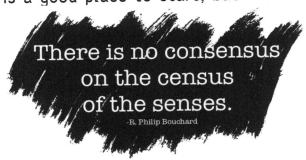

There is no consensus on the census of the senses.

-R. Philip Bouchard

Feeling with skin might deal with touch or temperature, gravity, or acceleration. Let's keep it simple as we're learning to feel. Four things that have helped me:

1. If something looks good, touch it. (I learned this by making friends with interior designers — they see with their fingertips).

2. Go to the gym (or a yoga class). For me, looking in the mirror to see what muscles are working changed what I felt.

3. Buy a fountain pen. Writing with a different tool changes the feel and somehow the thoughts.

What's helped you feel different?

FEELING BY HEART (OR SOUL)

We have to deal with "what is" when it comes to the other feelings too. Here are 3 things that have helped me:

1. Put it in words. Often we feel emotions, but don't see them because we don't name them.

2. See a therapist. There is a ton of baggage attached to emotions, a good counselor can help you unpack those bags.

3. Doodle the face — this is one of my favorites, so lets try it.

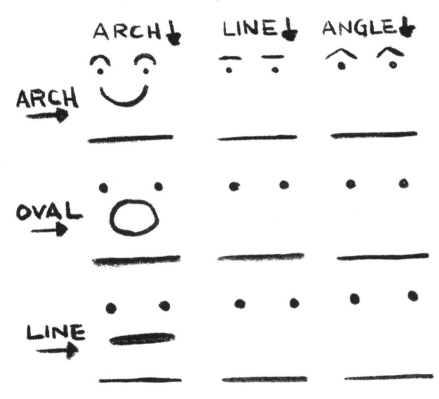

What has helped you?

idea FIVE
WHAT CAN BE

His grade school teacher asked what he'd been up too — we'll call her Mrs. Smith. Tom reminded her about the Air Force Academy and explained after graduation he became a fighter pilot. She pulled an envelope out of her stack; she had one for every student.

Tom remembered the drawing and the day. When asked, "What do you want to be when you grow up?" He'd stretched his arms out and exclaimed, "A jet plane!"

All the kids laughed and Mrs. Smith explained "people can't be planes." Then, Tom pivoted to fighter pilot.

It took work to even get into the Air Force Academy, they only have an 11% acceptance rate. After that, 20% drop out before reaching the half way point. Some say Tom had what it took, but the reality is he worked hard to get where he was.

What did you dream about as a child?

What can be? What do you dream about now?

Mrs. Smith was amazed at how many children drew pictures that were very close to what they were doing as adults. When I heard about Tom, I couldn't help but wonder what would have happened if he hadn't been told, "people can't be planes."

Ra has taught us to dream small. To see what can be, we need to embrace the creative spirit.

A Tom & Jerry is a lot like an egg nog, but you separate the eggs. It was Walt Disney's favorite holiday drink; the serving dish is still on the counter of his Disneyland apartment.

McNair was the Imagineer who: 1. sketched Disney Sea on the back of a bar napkin, 2. named "Downtown Disney" by writing it on a bathroom mirror, and 3. in the late 90's taught me how to juggle. When McNair put together a creative team, they came up with such great ideas that Disney bought out his contract, so they could hire him to teach his creative system.[42] The first step, my guess he lifted it from Walt's fondness for Tom & Jerry, separate two eggs.

Sensing "what is" is all about critical thinking.
Sensing "what can be" is creative thinking.

Sensing "what will be" is what we'll get to in separate, remember:

see,   say,   separate...
it's critical thinking again.

In a *tov* world, anything you separate is divided to dance. You can't get the stiff peaks on egg whites, unless you separate them from the yolks first. You can't see "what can be" until you shift from critical to creative thinking.

YES, AND...

The first rule of improv comedy is "Yes, &..."

"Yes," affirms whatever was said, and as we think about what can be, we need some affirmation. It's a lot easier to see all the bad things that can happen.

"&..." adds to it, expands it, multiplies it.... makes room in our minds for *tov*. "Yes, &.."

Take one thing that you know can be and write it in the middle circle then "yes, &..." to the other circles.

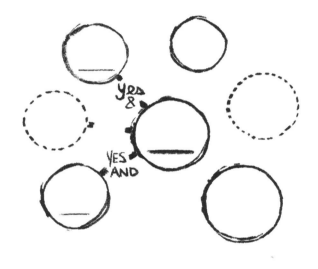

mORE IDEAS

What else?

We block creativity all the time. McNair has a "no blocking" rule. If you block someone else's idea, you put a buck in the blocking bowl (Yes, it's an actual fine). If you say, "I'm not blocking," that's blocking that your blocking, so the fine is $5. Another organization calls it "fire hosing," because one comment can quench the creative fire. Everyone in the room has a squirt gun, if you fire hose you get sprayed.

So what else can you be?

If you need a blocking bowl:[43] we set one up at www.FindYourTOV.com/blockingbowl.

!@%$ IDEAS

What are the ideas that make you blush? That are too expensive? That would never work? What wouldn't get committee approval?

What would be "sinful?" When we are thinking about *tov* we need to be acutely aware of the potential for Ra — that's another reason to come up with $@!•^& ideas when it comes to "What can be?" —-they count too.

You've got plenty of room...

How about 5 more.

REMEMBER THE MUDDLE

We've got to see "what is" before we see "what can be" or pick "what will be" — but, there's a muddle in the middle. Seeing comes before saying, but we need a vocabulary for vision.

Even when we have vocabulary, it's hard to see sometimes. We need to stop and sabbath. You won't see without Sabbath.

117

MOVEMENT IV
SABBATH

119

idea ONE

LOOK ONWARD

June Carter may have gotten Johnny Cash to return and reclaim his Christian roots, but when he sang, "got the number 13 tattooed on my neck,"[44] he was covering Danzing.[45]

We'll get to the semiotics of 13 next movement, it has everything to do with who you say what to when, but has a bad reputation. So many people fear this number triskaidekaphobia is an actual word. The only number with a worse reputation than is 666. It may seem odd, but the sign of the beast is a great place to start a section on Sabbath.

EVERY SYMBOL HAS A STORY

Seven means wholeness or completeness. Even Vegas tips its hat to holiness, calling it, "lucky number seven."

The story of seven starts, "in the beginning."[46] God set up a work/rest pattern by making the world in six working days, then taking a day of rest. 6+1=7...a complete week.

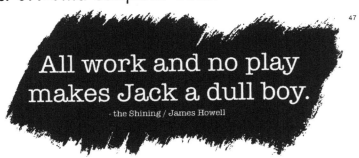

All work and no play makes Jack a dull boy.
- the Shining / James Howell [47]

Without a work/rest rhythm, 6-1-6-1-6-1 becomes work, work, work or 666. For me, when it was all work and no play (or rest), I didn't just become dull, life was hell.

My biggest regret is single handedly growing a High School group ministry in Grapevine, Texas, from 4 to 70 in a couple years. I was proudly putting in more than a hundred hours each week, missed the first three years of Kaitlyn's life, almost ruined my marriage, and ended up with a bleeding ulcer. My life was a living hell, a connected chain of sixes.

Balance is boring, stagnant, a lot harder and less productive than flow (the Divided To Dance concept in MOVEMENT VI dives into this). Still, work/life balance is a great societal step toward Sabbath, so let's roll with it. From nonexistent to nailing it, how is your work/life balance?

nonexistent   nailing it

0 - - 1 - - 2 - - 3 - - 4 - - 5 - - 6 - - 7 - - 8 - - 9 - - 10

Some people like to circle a number, others need some space to expalin why, so here you go.

666 is a pattern broken by Sabbath. When is your Sabbath, one day each week where you aren't define by what you do?

If you don't have one, when could it be?

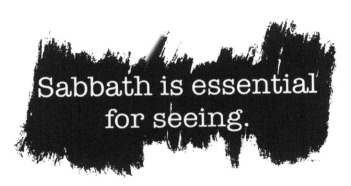

Sabbath is essential for seeing.

That's why the Sabbath Movement is here between see and say, but if you don't have a rhythm of rest, start slow. Maybe you need to pencil in a morning off each week. Take a morning for a month before you move to a half day, then a full Sabbath. For most of us, it's about reclaiming a rhythm. The first step, 0 to 1, is alwaysthe hardest.

Just like

It's better to walk a mile
than sit on the couch
thinking about how you should
be running a 5K[48]

It's better to start by taking a morning off than shame yourself for not Sabbathing.

Pressing pause for one day each week will help us remember not just who, but whose we are. Unfortunately, most of us have been trained to think about our worth in terms of what we do, rather than who we are. We've been taught to rest from work rather than work from rest. That's why, after a vacation, it's pretty common to burn up on reentry.

It is essential to look at not burning up on reentry, looking at 6, rather than fearing it.

FORMING AND FILLING

The pattern isn't just 6+1=7, but 3+3=6 (or 2½ + 3 ½ = 6 to be more precise). Work, at least fruitful *tov* work, is forming and filling.

 Day One[49] is called Day One not "the first day" because it's all about forming a "day"—one light and one dark. There's a rest and work rhythm built in each day.

The second day,[50] the language changes from one, two, three (cardinal) to first, second, third (ordinal) and is forming the sky and the sea, although the "water below isn't named until the mud is separated. In the evening of the third day[51] (days started in the evening) the land and sea are formed.

First there was forming.

God saw what was, what could be, and picked what would be, then made containers for it. After things were formed, filling is inevitable.

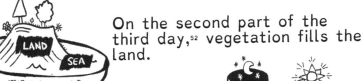

On the second part of the third day,[52] vegetation fills the land.

The fourth day,[53] sun fills Day One and overflows into the second day.

Likewise, the fifth day[54] fowl fill the second day sky and fish overflow to fill the third day.

Finally, the sixth day[55] land creatures fill the third day land and...

people overflow to forming[56] the next week.

It's this pattern of work, forming and filling, that is called very *tov*.[57] But we have to rest well before we can work well.

We are in the middle, millennia into the story, so there is bound to be a muddle. We start by looking onward, to set the Sabbath, even though our vision will flow from it.

If we rest from work, rather than work from rest, it's easy to lose sight of what we are doing. How often do you look back and wonder what happened to the day?

You are tired, but wonder what was accomplished. It's easy to flip forming and filling. We can be busy with a whole lot of nothing. It's actually worse than most people think. Set out to do 2 or 3 things, you'll get 2 or 3 things accomplished.[58]

A "To-Do" list is the first step to forming. What's on yours this week?

TO DO

1. _____

2. _____

3. _____

You may have gotten used to blank pages and extra room, but not here. If you set out to do 4–10 things, you'll only accomplish 1 or 2 of them. When we raise our to do list to 11–20, nothing gets accomplished.

Most people, like most organizations, have lists with 11–20 things on them, some have 20+.

In **MOVEMENT VI: SEPARATE**, we'll do a deep dive into what to chip away to get to those magic 2 or 3 things. Sometimes its best to flip there now.

For now, let's take the first step. If you aren't already taking a Sabbath when will it be?

[ ] Sunday

[ ] Monday

[ ] Tuesday

[ ] Wednesday

[ ] Thursday

[ ] Friday

[ ] Saturday

Is your next right thing forming

[ ] 2 hours for Sabbath

if so when will it be? (_____ to _____)

[ ] Half Day

if so when will it be? (_____ to _____)

[ ] Full 24 Hours

if so when does it start?

I suggest at least a month at each of these before you try to step it up. If you are just starting, it's not uncommon to take a season (3-4 months) to get into the practice of Sabbath. That's why we left the rest of this movment and an entire other movement before SEPARATE.

Today, Sabbath demands you look onward to: see it, form it, and fill it. In the end it allows us to look onward, more clearly seeing what's ahead. From rest we look onward to something better than work. It orften feels more like play because it's living our *tov*. To get there, we have to press pause first, and often.

It doesn't matter if you are taking two hours, half a day, or a full day. We need to LOOK ONWARD and ask, "What needs to happen before Sabbath, so you can Sabbath better?"

For a season, we made a crock-pot meal Friday so we wouldn't have to cook Saturday (our Sabbath).

LOOK DOWN

Maybe it was culture shock. I'd never needed a passport before this trip, but sitting on the floor of Paul and Elly's home, eating spaghetti with new friends seemed normal enough; However, our conversation didn't.

Paul pointed out pressing pause, was counter cultural for Americans. Since I was the only one in the house without a British accent, the spotlight was on me.

Unfortunately, I couldn't argue. The doc who told me I had a bleeding ulcer said the same thing.

Sadly, the church was rewarding me for overwork. They should have fired me. After all, the Bible puts not taking a day off right up there with murder in God's top 10 list of sins.

Over the years, as a student of Sabbath, this is what I've learned:

If you don't STOP, you won't SEE.

Sabbath is a particular way to press pause, a certain kind of rest. Forming Sabbath, really setting yourself up for success, is all about looking in four directions.

To Sabbath well, before it starts,

LOOK DOWN and ask, "Where am I?"

then LOOKBACK and ask, "What happened?" (or "How'd I get here?)

This sets you up for success so you know how to rest. In the midst of Sabbath

LOOK UP asking, "What is the bigger story being told?"

Finally, as Sabbath comes to an end
LOOK ONWARD

 deciding what you will do next, because SEE flows from Sabbath.

Sometimes, religious people get hung up on when sabbath is. In Jesus day, they argued with him about it. Truth is, it doesn't matter when Sabbath happens, but that it does. For the last decade, as a Pastor, my Monday (the first day of the working week) was Sunday, so my Friday night (when my weekend started), was Thursday night.

Thursday morning, when I tell a barista, "Have a good weekend," they look at me a bit strange, but they get it. Restaurants and theaters are dark Monday, so Sunday is their Friday. Baristas are in "the industry," so they figure it out quickly.

The day doesn't matter, but whenever your Friday is, start with a Look Down.

Where are you?

What do you see?

Are your sensible shoes still planted behind a desk as the sun sets, or have you traded them for stilettos, sneakers, or sandals? Is sand or sod beneath your feet — hardwood, carpet, or pavement? Can you see your feet, or is your belly blocking your view? Taking a moment to look down can be a game changer. Whether we like it or not, it tells us what is.

130

Most of us carry phones, so set an alarm for 5:00pm Friday (whenever that is for you). Don't just look down, take a picture too. Sometimes, we have to capture to see.

Doodling forces me to slow down. If I know I'm blowing over the "where am I question," I capture it with a doodle, just to slow down. Give it a try.

CAPTURE

Someday, I'll figure out if it is "stop and see," or "stop to see." Lately I've been leaning toward both. Either one works, as long as we do it. I carry a little 3.5"x5.5" notebook with me almost everywhere I go because I've learned this much if I don't stop, I won't see.

The shortest pencil is longer than the longest memory.
-Mark Batterson

Sometimes, words are the best way to capture, but you've got a vocabulary bigger than just words; maybe it's just five "letters:"

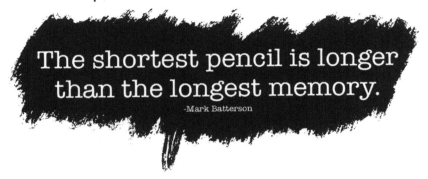

DOT   LINE   ANGLE   ARCH   SQUIGGLE   OVAL

Maybe your vocabulary calls point instead of dot. I added squiggle and dropped the rest, perhaps

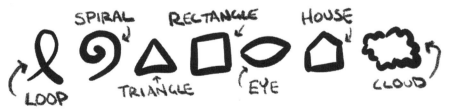

LOOP   SPIRAL   TRIANGLE   RECTANGLE   EYE   HOUSE   CLOUD

are in your arsenal too. You've got the vocabulary to have a vision — so look down and capture it.

I'm convinced a big reason everybody can draw in the first grade, but by third grade it's down to one-third of the class, is we teach busy-ness. Drawing requires the do nothing day Sabbath gives us — so fill this page....

... and this one too.

Eyes are great for capturing some things. Where you are physically is one of them. If you can't see your feet because of of your belly, that tells you something. Maybe you've been eating too many sweets, or just too much. Perhaps your excerise routine has slipped. Then again, it might be lack of sleep and high cortisol levels and the belly is a hint you need to deal with some emotional stuff. It's not a strength (physical) issue, but soul (emotional) one.

Carpe Diem means seize the day. Drawing, or doodling, is not the goal or the end — capturing is. If drawing isn't working, grab a camera (or the app on your phone) and take a shot. Remember,

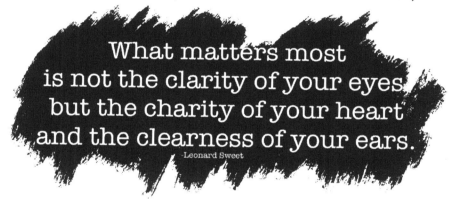

What matters most
is not the clarity of your eyes
but the charity of your heart
and the clearness of your ears.
-Leonard Sweet

If that looks familiar, this quote was back on page 101. Yes, you've seen it already.

Looking down gives us hints at "what is." When, "what is" isn't visual, our eyes aren't helpful.

In ancient times (and I'd argue still today) the greatest command was to love with all our heart, soul, strength, and mind. When we look down, it's helpful to see (or sense) where our heart, soul, strength and mind are — not just our feet.

HEART

Back then, heart was the seat of the will.[59] To love with all of your heart was to make a choice to love. When we look down at our heart, we ask:

Am I doing what I want to be doing?

What choices are lining up with who I want to be and where I want to go?"

Which choices are taking me somewhere else?

Whenever your Friday is, take a moment and capture where your heart is.

SOUL

Nowdays, its unclear what people mean when they say soul. I don't know what a soul looks like, so I drew the bottom of my foot. Back in the day, when people wanted to talk about emotions they talked about **SOUL** (or guts). This makes sense, when I'm with Tricia my heart still skips a beat, but she also gives me butterflies in my tummy.

Where is your soul, right now?

How are you emotionally? Take a moment to look down and capture it.

Whenever your Friday is, take a moment and capture your soul (deep emotions).

STRENGTH

Strength is about your physical body, and by extension your resources.

A few years back, I started working with a trainer. He wouldn't just have me weigh in, but would measure my chest, arms, and legs, on a regular basis. This trainer knew my workouts. If I was in the gym, he was watching, but also asked about what I was eating and how I was sleeping.

Likewise, when I sat down with a friend to help with budgeting, the first thing we did was look down and see how much was coming in, how much was going out, and most importantly, where it was going.

Where is your strength (resources)? Are your resources energized, exhausted, or somewhere in between? What do you want to be capturing and how will you capture it?

Whenever your Friday is, take a moment and capture your strength (resources).

MIND

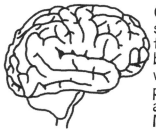

Capturing where my soul and strength are is something I try to do every week. I used to blame **ADHD**, but even people who don't have it need to pause more than once a week and capture their thoughts. Maybe a look down and capture your soul or strength daily would work better for you too. For me, checking my **MIND** is best done daily — then I review it on your Friday.

Where's my mind been _____day?
What have you been thinking about?

Where's my mind been _____day?
What have you been thinking about?

Where's my mind been _____day?
What have you been thinking about?

Pay attention to what you pay attention to.

-Amy Krouse Rosenthall

Where's my mind been _____day?
What have you been thinking about?

Where's my mind been _____day?
What have you been thinking about?

Where's my mind been _____day?
What have you been thinking about?

140

When I **LOOK BACK** (idea four), I have something to look back at. Also at the end of Sabbath, I capture it too. Where's my mind been this Sabbath? What have I been thinking about?

You can't connect the dots
LOOKING FORWARD;
you can only connect them
LOOKING BACKWARDS.
So you have to trust that the dots
will somehow connect in the future.
YOU HAVE TO TRUST SOMETHING.

-Steve Jobs

READY, SET, STOP

Kaitlyn graduated from college in 2019. She and I got to visit China over her Spring Break, but didn't realize New Year began that year on February 5. Since they celebrate for almost 3 weeks (think the Christmas break in America) they were just getting back to normal when we were there. They had ushered in 4717 the year of the Boar.

Adeline was in Cincinnati when I was in Israel. She had a bowel perforation and was being rushed into surgery. Since it was Rosh Hashanah, everything was closed, including airports. If you are Jewish, that's your New Year. What I called 2017 was 5778 on the Jewish calendar. They are looking back to Adam and Eve, for year 1.

Gregorian calendar looks back to Jesus. AD means *anno domina*, "the year of our Lord" in Latin. Whatever your culture, New Year has a date attached, a built in reminder, to look back.

After we look down and ask, "Where am I?" It's helpful to look back, asking, "How'd I get here?" It only takes two questions to set you up for success. They are the ready and set before you stop.

Before we look back, we need to decide what we are looking back to. How far are we looking back?

Gabe McCauley, the host of Reconnecting Roots,[61] wears a Slow-watch.[62] It has only one hand and all 24 hours are numbered on the face. Before I saw it, I thought a watch needed an hour, minute, and second hand, but do you ever say 6:18, or do you round to 6:20?

Slow-watch works. They are more a philosophy than a product. Gabe takes the long view when he looks back and this is reflected in his show.

Wherever you are on this planet, one day means being in the same spot in relation to the sun again. To get there takes light (day) and dark (night). Long before my daughters could tell time they understood this, so Tricia would tell them "Dad will be back after 3 more darks." Day dancing with night is the primary way we organize time.

Benjamin Franklin was first a print maker, so he recorded what he did with his time. Mason Currey introduces us to the "daily rituals"[63] of Ben Franklin and 160 other "inspired — and inspiring — minds." How they fill one light and one dark is truly *miyn*, that's of its kind, but each person had regular rhythms of rest and work.

What does your "normal weekday" look like?

This is what Ben Franklin's looked like

The morning question, What good shall I do this day?	5	Rise, wash, and address *Powerful Goodness;* contrive day's business and take the resolution of the day; prosecute the present study; and breakfast.
	6	
	7	
	8	
	9	Work.
	10	
	11	
	12	Read or overlook my accounts, and dine.
	1	
	2	Work.
	3	
	4	
	5	
	6	Put things in their places, supper, music, or diversion, or conversation; examination of the day.
	7	
	8	
	9	
Evening question, What good have I done today?	10	
	11	
	12	
	1	Sleep.
	2	
	3	
	4	

At least that's how he laid out the pages. My guess is that was his ideal work day, not his every day.

What would your "ideal weekday" be?

Julian Cameron helps people recapture creativity. One of the biggest tools she uses is Morning Pages, "Put simply, the morning pages are three pages of longhand writing, strictly stream-of-consciousness."[64] When I started Morning Pages, it was only a 40 minute change to my day (many people say 15, but they take me 40). It was a 40 minute step toward the ideal. Looking at your ideal day, what is one step you can make in the next 24 hours (one dark and one light)?

As much as I wanted Morning Pages to be a time to look back, they couldn't be. They were a great way to look down and capture where I was. Being close enough to capture doesn't give the distance needed to looking back. Maybe, Ben Franklin got at it with his evening question, but I needed more space.

Most people do.

If you don't STOP,
you won't SEE.

God's top ten commandment list has "take a day off" on it. It's listed right up there with don't murder, cheat on your spouse, or steal. More specifically, the commandment is:

> Remember the Sabbath day, to keep it holy. Six days you shall labor and do all your work, but the seventh day is the sabbath of the LORD thy God — thou shall not do any work— not thy son, nor thy daughter, nor thy manservant, not thy maidservant, nor thy cattle, not thy stranger in your gate.[65]

A day off is that important. If your whole family is doing it, a weekly Sabbath gives us a built in rhythm of rest. A time far enough removed from the one dark and one light rhythm that we can look back and see something, but close enough our memory hasn't gotten fuzzy.

Look back 25 pages (idea **ONE** on page 124). When is your weekly Sabbath?

Most people engage an idea each week, so you are likely finding a weekly rhythm.

Sabbath isn't just about a weekly rhythm though. On the fourth day, when God filled the sky with stars, they were signs.

> God said, "Let there be lights — in the expanse of the heavens to separate the day from the night. And let them be signs for seasons, and for days, and for years.[66]

A sign is never about itself, but points to something else. We've already unpacked days — one night and one dark, but what about seasons?

SEASONS GET LOST IN THE SHUFFLE

Christmas happens next to Winter Solstice, but takes over stores the day after Halloween. Winter, Spring, Summer, and Fall, are marked by the stars, particularly the big one we call Sun.

Twice a year the sun stands still — at least that's what solstice means (*sol* is Latin for sun, *sistere* — to stand still).

Winter Solstice (December 21/22) is the longest dark (shortest light) of the year. If you've went around the sun a few times you know what's coming. Six months later, (June 21/22) it's flipped. Summer Solstice is the longest light and shortest dark. These are built in signs to look back a little further.

What do the solstice signs point to for you?

Do you have ways you mark the seasons that are working?

If so, celebrate and solidify them.
If not, what could it look like?

I suggest a 3 day / 2 night retreat twice a year.

Winter Solstice
December 21/22

Summer Solstice
June 21/22

LOOK DOWN Where are you?

Where is your **SOUL (DEEP EMOTIONS)?**

Where is your **STRENGTH (RESOURCES)?**

Where is your **MIND?**

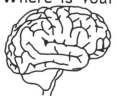

Maybe you start with this, maybe you play for a few hours first. Then it's one dark.
After a good night's rest, sometimes with more playing beforehand, the day is dedicated to LOOK BACK and LOOK UP.

LOOK BACK and reflect on with 3 HEART (WILL) questions.

Are you where you wanted to be?

Either way, if you are where you wanted to be, or if you are not, the next questions are why. If you are where you wanted to be, why? (what worked?). If you aren't, why? What happened?

The third question, "What did I learn?" flows into LOOK UP because there is always a bigger story being told. For me, part of this is journaling, praying, thinking. I also eat a lot, walk a lot, and end up taking a nap or two this day.

After another sleep the morning of the third day is dedicated to **LOOK FORWARD**. We'll dive into this in the next idea: **LOOK BACK / MOVE FORWARD**. There aren't just two seasons, there are four. We don't want to forget

Spring Equinox
March 20/21

Fall Equinox
September 22/23

Alexander Shaia encourages pilgrims who walk the Camino de Santiago, "Stay at your turn-around-place from a few days to a week or longer."[67] In bygone days people walked to Santiago, Muxia, or Fisterre, then walked home, so the turn-around-point was built in. What was a turn-around-place, is now the destination as today's pilgrims head home to trains and planes. Heat and air conditioning, as well electric lights, can have the same effect on Solstice, our planets turn-around-places.

Spring starts on March 20/21 and Fall September 22/23. These are the moments the light and dark are equal, hence equinox. It's a subtle shift from the days getting shorter to the nights getting longer. How are you using these times to "mark the seasons?" If you aren't how could you be?

MORE THAN SEASONS

In the same way, every seventh day should be a Sabbath day, Leviticus says:

Six years you shall sow your fields, and six years you shall prune your vineyards and gather fruits, but the seventh year shall be a Sabbath of rest for the Land, a Sabbath to the LORD: don't sow the field, or prune the vine.[68]

Stefan Sagmeister is a rockstar in the graphic design world, complete with loud leather jacket and autograph seeking groupies. He is not a religious person, but is the first person I've met who lives this Leviticus passage.

In his Ted Talk, two images made his point. We spend about our first 25 years learning, the next 40 working, then "tacked on at the end are about 15 years of retirement."[69]

He "basically cut off, five retirement years and interspersed them into those working years."

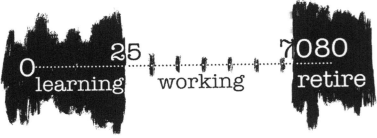

What would you do if you had a year to press pause?

Remember: No blocking

153

idea FOUR

LOOK BACK / MOVE FORWARD

Dad never needed rear view mirrors. He had a sixth sense when it came to changing lanes, but he learned the importance of looking back when he got a call from a post office in a town he'd never been to.

The day they called, dad was driving a semi-truck from Indiana to California,[70] and making great time. Colorado mountain passes weren't slowing him down at all. For the last couple hours, his truck seemed lighter...because it was.

Somehow, his trailer had detached, rolled backward down a hill and through the wall of the post office. Since Dad owned the company, it was his phone number printed on the side of the trailer. Until they called, since it wasn't his habit to look back, he didn't notice the trailer was gone, until that call.

Plenty of property was damaged, but thankfully no one was hurt. Insurance covered the cost, but even if they hadn't, the lesson: "look back to move forward," would have been worth the price.

One definition of insanity, is doing the same thing and expecting a different result. If we never look back, we don't know what we did or how we got to where we are. That makes it very hard to change anything.

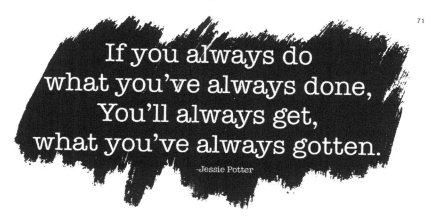

If you always do
what you've always done,
You'll always get,
what you've always gotten.

-Jessie Potter

At the end of the week (or sometimes season), it's not uncommon to look down and realize "I'm exhausted." There is nothing right or wrong about sketching a fuel gauge on E, as a way to capture where my strength is.

It's also not that interesting. The sketch doesn't tell me enough.

For a season, I was in the gym every morning by 3:30am, so I could be writing when the coffee shop opened at 5:00am. Looking back and seeing a few late night meetings told me how I got too tired — so, Sabbath was not setting an alarm and planning a nap. Looking back helped me move forward.

Other weeks my tank was on the same E, but tired came from the exact opposite reason. I was getting plenty of sleep, but absolutely no exercise. Looking back to move forward helped me see sabbath rest sometimes looks like a long jog.

While rest has a rhythm, if we mindlessly move into it, without first looking back, we fall into a rut rather than finding a groove.

What we do for a day each season, we do in a few minutes each Friday. Look back.... What happened last week to get you to your "what is?"

HEART   SOUL

STRENGTH   MIND

"Think before you drink," is a tag line in recovery. HALT (hungry, angry, lonely, tired) is the acronym that goes along with it. If you are hungry, reach for a sandwich not a bottle, lonely– call a friend, tired– take a nap. You don't need to be in recovery to address what you really need.

After looking down (asking, "Where am I?") and looking back (asking, "What happened to get me here?") put the pieces together and ask, "What's next?"

As I step into sabbath, what would refresh my soul (emotion)?

As I step into sabbath what would restore my strength?

As I step into sabbath what would renew my mind?

There are no "right" answers, only real ones.

Maybe, you noticed a question missing. For most people dealing with heart/will, or what we want, is a work thing. So, like creative and critical thinking, (back on day 5: See) we separate the eggs.

Heart is all about form.

When will you form your week?

MOVING FORWARD

Do you remember getting a plastic protractor at back to school time? I'd lose mine long before we'd get to that chapter and have to borrow one. Our teacher always had a box of extra supplies other students had left behind. Numbers were there, but the paint had been rubbed off. Since the worksheets were the same year after year, those tick marks were completely worn off too, I learned to estimate.

Years later, a pilot told me never to estimate angles. There is a rule of 60 in navigation. For every 60 miles you travel, you'll be one mile off your destination for every degree you are off.

Two degrees off may seem like nothing, but even though Chicago is 25 miles from north to south, you'd miss the entire city flying from New York. In the same way that it's great to capture a day (look down), but fruitless to look back every day, its really tough to look onward every week. Seasonally, however, look onward and then make sure you aren't too many degrees off every week.

I use the 5 capitals.

Where do you want to be financially this season?

What do I want to learn this season?

Where do I want to be physically by the end of this season?

What relationships do I need to invest in this season?

Where do I want to be spiritually at the end of this season?

Once I've drawn a line from where I am to where I want to be in a week or a season, it makes it a lot easier to look back weekly and adjust for any degrees I'm off.

idea FIVE:
PLAY THE LONG GAME

For over two decades, since our apartment with a one butt kitchen, a Monopoly board has followed us. When DJ Khaled dropped *All I Do Is Win*, Emma Stone wasn't the only one lip syncing. (If you haven't seen this go to youtube now.) What I'm getting at is Tricia and I are both competitive.

When we met, she was on the tennis team. The next year, she took home the NCAA double championship trophy with her partner. Notice I never said Tricia *played* tennis. There was *hitting around* and the *match*, even the word *game* served as a stepping stone to winning — game, set, match.

No college sports for me, but I was all the more competitive. For some reason, Monopoly brought out the worst in us and to avoid divorce, 1998 is the last time we competed. (Tricia's name is next to the date, so I guess she won.)

Often, you've got to stop competing if you want to play.

When was the last time you played, not competed, but played?

Play, both as a noun and a verb, is an engagement in activity "for enjoyment and recreation."[73] Even though "I want to play Monopoly," is the first example when you google "play definition," we get the point.

Adam and Eve worked, rested, and played in the garden, but when I read it, Genesis 3, it seems like God only cursed work. When we work there will be struggle, when it comes to rest and play, it seems to be a different story. Len Sweet famously refused to work at his marriage and instead played at it.[74] That's some good advice.

As you **LOOK BACK** to **MOVE FORWARD**, what do you need to start playing at?

Sonnets in the **SEE** movement, and haiku too, have an ulterior motive. They flirt with play. Poetry depends on wordplay. (Don't miss that wordPLAY). Even if you don't like rap, you can't dismiss Jay **Z**'s expertise at wordplay.

When it comes to wordplay the prefix "re" is mine. Everyone has a favorite toy. Play is synonomous with recreation. Add a colon, and recreation becomes re:creation. Play is defined as "concerning creation." Add a dash, and re-creation means play is where things get created again, and again, and again. No wonder play helps us see *tov*.

When it comes to work, more sales mean more stress, but when it comes to toys, more is just more.

What was your favorite toy growing up?

Is there a toy you wish you had today?

Someday, I'll save up $800 and buy the 7,541 piece Millennium Falcon from Lego. Currently, Tricia and I are putting together the Lego World Map, which has the most pieces (11,695), but it's more 2D than 3D — when it comes to play we are drawn to depth.

By the way, Jay Z doesn't really play with words, Shawn Carter does. He owns his moniker as an alter ego and the verses as embellishments.[75]

In movies, and in rap, people PLAY characters Live theater goes a step further, and calls the thing that's going on, a play.

Sometimes on vacation I go by Hank, Hank Sabbatical. This isn't an alter ego, but a reminder to play – to recreate and be recreated. What would your sabbath name be?

As competive as we are, Tricia and I got to know each other during *Godspell*.[76] Play, or at least a play, is our foundation. The point of a play is to tell a different, often bigger story and and let actors play pretend.

Donald Miller learned how to see a bigger picture when he helped turn a memoir he wrote about himself, into a screen-play (aka movie). After changing his life and sharing it in *A Million Miles in a Thousand Years*,[77] he helps companies do the same thing. This is play, at work.

My favorite birthdays, Tricia has taken me to plays. One of them was *Rent*.[78] In *Seasons of Love*[79] they reframe a year as "five hundred twenty-five thousand, six hundred minutes." This play, like all plays, call to LOOK UP and see each minute as part of something so much bigger.

Play, by definition is fun. We laugh and talk and dream. Or as Taylor Swift sings

> It seems like one of those nights
> When we ditch the whole scene
> And end up dreaming' instead of sleeping[80]

Yes, Sabbath is about rest (sleeping), but it's also about play (dreaming). In it, we sense new adventures. We know we are part of something bigger, and begin to see with eyes of faith.

Once we **SEE**, we've got to **SHARE**.

MOVEMENT V
SAY

169

idea ONE
WORDS DO THINGS

Getting married is weird. Maybe it's different in other states, but in Indiana, the couple goes to the courthouse, pays $25 ($65 if either lives out of state). Then, in front of a county clerk, sign a marriage license.

They both signed, the clerk put a seal on it, but they aren't married.

Sometime in the next 60 days the wedding has to happen or the license expires and all that was for nothing. My job as an officiant was to sign that paper. When I do, they are married. Except, the court won't know I signed. For a few days, the marriage is in the mail. After that, it will take some time to process the paperwork.

I asked a lawyer friend when they were really married. Turns out, when I said, "I now pronounce you" the deed is done. J.L. Austin says, "Performative utterance is not, or not merely, saying something but doing something."[81]

More simply, words do things. When the officiant says they are married, they are.

Remember the chiasm

> God said,   "Let there be light."
>> God saw the light is *tov*
> God separated the light from the darkness.[82]

Light hadn't been separated from darkness yet, but the words "and there was light," show up after said, not separated. As poet and podcaster Propaganda puts it:

[83]

+ (POSITIVE) & – (NEGATIVE)

Negative things stick with us more than positive things. Research has proven that to live a "positive life" more than three times as many positive things have to happen than negative ones.[84]

Words are even more weighty. Harrison Friedman studied couples playing board games. The ones that had "long term happiness"[85] also made five positive comments for every one negative.[86]

My second grade music teacher, Mrs. Barnes would make us say three "build ups" if she ever heard a "put down." She knew the power of performative words.

Look back. When has someone told you that you were really good at something?

What did they "speak into existence?"

Years into adulthood, many people are still holding onto negative words, especially ones they heard as children. One woman, a virgin until she married, had issues around sex because a respected uncle told her dress made her look slutty. She was six. The hardest worker I've ever met believed he was lazy, and recounted the day his dad spoke those words to him. Countless brilliant people believe they are stupid because someone spoke that reality into existence.

What negative words are you still carrying around, even though they aren't true?

Justin was part of the writers group I met with at Old Crown every Wednesday night for years. He put it this way:

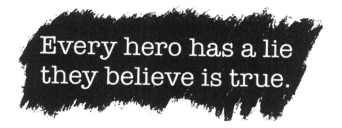

Every hero has a lie they believe is true.

For most of us, someone somewhere spoke that lie into existence. That's the power of words. Calling a lie what it is, speaks something into existence too. That's why what Marianne Williamson said echoes and gets attributed to Nelson Mandela.

> Our deepest fear is not that we are inadequate. Our deepest fear is that we are powerful beyond measure. It is our light, not our darkness that most frightens us. We ask ourselves, 'Who am I to be brilliant, gorgeous, talented, fabulous?' Actually, who are you not to be? You are a child of God. Your playing small does not serve the world. There is nothing enlightened about shrinking so that other people won't feel insecure around you. We are all meant to shine, as children do. We were born to make manifest the glory of God that is within us. It's not just in some of us; it's in everyone. And as we let our own light shine, we unconsciously give other people permission to do the same. As we are liberated from our own fear, our presence automatically liberates others.[87]

Like all words, her words create worlds. I don't care who told you different, but someone needs to hear this — you are brilliant, gorgeous, talented, fabulous. You are *tov!*

Take a moment, what did those words stir up in you?

A "performative utterance" doesn't need to be formal or official. Informality may be where the power of words come from. It would take a special kind of *Ra* to premeditate calling a child stupid or lazy, but it happens.

A couple thousands of years before academics like J. L. Austen talked about words doing things, James wrote:

> When we put bits into the mouths of horses to make them obey us, we can turn the whole animal. Or take ships as an example. Although they are so large and are driven by strong winds, they are steered by a very small rudder wherever the pilot wants to go. Likewise, the tongue is a small part of the body, but it makes great boasts. Consider what a great forest is set on fire by a small spark. The tongue also is a fire, a world of evil among the parts of the body. It corrupts the whole body, sets the whole course of one's life on fire, and is itself set on fire by hell.
>
> All kinds of animals, birds, reptiles and sea creatures are being tamed and have been tamed by mankind, but no human being can tame the tongue. It is a restless evil, full of deadly poison.[88]

The good news is, naming the untruth can undo its hold.

IMAGO DEI

In Latin, God created people *imago dei*.[89] There's a ring to the Latin. It feels fancy and formal, but *imago dei* just means "in the image of God." Something about you, and everyone you meet, reflects divinity.

When "God said, 'Let there be light,'"[90] the sentence continues with "and there was light," but something still had to be done. A couple sentences later, the work of separating, pulling the the light from the darkness, began. However, once it's said, it is.

Even before the work something exists. There are no take backs when it comes to words.

As kids we had spelling bees. Spelling is how words are made. When witches cast spells they are testifying to words doing things. They might have a better grasp on the creative power of words than other groups.

Calling letters,
    that spell words,
    that do things,
"magic" sounds oddly accurate, doesn't it?

Words are *tov*. As such, they have potential to become *Ra*. Being dyslexic, I have to slow down to spell and often I do it wrong. Every obstacle can be an advantage. We can learn from witches and dyslexics. First remembering the magic of what we say, remember that words create worlds. Then, slow down and speak deliberately.

Back in 2001, the MTA in New York started using this slogan.

Years later, they licensed it to the Department of Homeland Security, but registering a slogan with the US Patent and Trademark Office doesn't make "see something, say something" new.

See then say, has been around since the beginning. The slogan brings up a question. Who do I say something to?

Who you say what to, and when, is often the difference between *tov* and *Ra*.

idea TWO
SIZE MATTERS

Everybody acts differently depending on who they are around. In 1963, an anthropologist called Edward T. Hall realized how physically close we were to each other told us about the relationship. Hall called his studies proxemics, and came up with four spaces.

INTIMATE SPACE happens when people are within 18 inches of each other.

If you don't think spatially, I'm 6 feet tall (3 inches above average). This makes the middle of my body 3 feet from my finger tip and puts my elbow at the 18 inch half way point. To share intimate space means you are close enough I can put my arm around you.

People act and interact a certain way when they are this close. As you think through your life who do you regularly get within 18 inches of?

Kids learn about "bubble space" for all sorts of reasons; dad not always being a jungle gym was a big one in our family. Space doesn't create a relationship, but it helps.

Our brains don't always think. When bodies are 18 inches away from each other, brains short circuit. Cosmetology school doesn't have a psychology class, but barbers and hairdressers become counselors because they share intimate space all day.

Even if you've never heard about proxemics, words create worlds. Giving something a name often means we are paying attention to it.

Kaitlyn lives in Orlando and designs themed environments. She mentioned she was going to "fifth wheel" to Magic Kingdom on her day off. I'd never heard that phrase before, so I asked. Two couples were going on a double date[91] and she was tagging along. Join a couple when they are on a date, you are a "third wheel," so joining a double date is being a "fifth wheel."

The fact you know what a "third wheel" is, means we know about intimate space (even if we don't know we know about it). Only one person at a time can fit in intimate space. I've got two arms, but can only focus on one thing at a time. Focus is another feature of intimate space.

Intimate Space means there is only one thing to focus on, the other person. Also, and probably more importantly, you are getting the full focus of the other person.

Another anthropologist, Robin Dunbar, didn't look at space but size.[92] Facebook lets you have 5,000 friends, even though you will only be able to recognize 1,500 of them, so we know the word friend has changed. Playground rules dictate you can only have one best friend. Like most things, the reality is somewhere in the middle.

In *the Message*, Eugene Peterson translates Proverbs 18:24 this way, "Friends come and friends go, but a true friend sticks by you like family." That's why it's so important to figure out who these people are. Who are yours?

1. _____   2. _____

3. _____   4. _____

5. _____

You don't need to have five, but you can't have more than five. I don't make the rules, your brain does and neurologists discover them.

A good friend will bail you out of jail,
but a best friend
will be sitting beside you saying,
"that was awesome."

-Kate Angell

PERSONAL SPACE

An iPhone in intimate space doesn't have to destroy the relationship, but it does change the space. When another person is in the space it shifts from intimate to personal space. It's not just iPhones, children do this too. When a couple has a child the family shifts from intimate to personal space.

Make note of times intimate space shifts to personal space. This isn't a bad thing, it's simply a change worth noting.

Before kids, I used to get 100% of Tricia's attention. Kaitlyn came along and when she was awake, the best I could hope for was 50%. Instead of one relationship (Tricia and I) there were three, and I wasn't even part of one of them (Tricia and Kaitlyn).

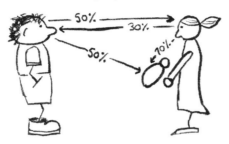

Drawing this out helped a bit, but it was still a lot to process. All of this happens when we shift from intimate space to personal space.

Hall noticed personal space happened when we were between 1½ and 4 feet from each other. Even though 18 inches and 1½ feet are the same distance the language changes. The shift is bigger than space.

I'd bet people who say, "I need some personal space" couldn't pick Edward T. Hall out of a lineup. They haven't studied proxemics, but important words creep into everyday language. Words do things, exposing reality is one of them.

Where do you find yourself needing personal space?

Paradoxically, for me, the line between what usually gets called kin (the five who are really good at sharing intimate space) and super family (what Dunbar calls the group of up to fifteen people closest to you), was distance. Long before I heard about Hall or Dunbar, I knew I had friends, and road friends.

Nathan danced with Tricia at my wedding, and took me out for a beer the night we buried my Dad. In our 20's, we played music together and drove a van from Thousand Oaks to Tacoma in our boxers because the air conditioning broke and we needed to make it to a wedding. Feelings aren't hurt if months go by without a text or call. He lives in Michigan, and I never have. When we are together we pick up where we left off.

We look to kin for support, super-family for sympathy.

My brother, technically step-brother, and I lived in a trailer park across the street from each other. We introduced our parents and shared a room for years. It felt icky to own that he had changed lists (from kin to super-family), but three decades seperated by hundred of miles will do that. When I was honest only three of my five kin spots were filled: Tricia, Kaitlyn, and Adeline — I don't have capacity for more intimacy than that.

It changes with age and stage

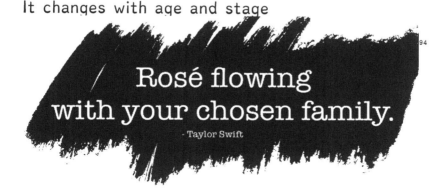

Rosé flowing with your chosen family.
- Taylor Swift

"Chosen family" is Taylor's way to get at the concept of kin. Maybe for you, distance isn't the line between kin and super-family, but what ever it is it's worth thinking about. Even more, important is taking stock of who they are:

6. _____   7. _____

8. _____   9. _____

10. _____   11. _____

12. _____   13. _____

14. _____   15. _____

My *alma mater* has a hashtag: #BeKnow. It took me 4 universities (and a decade) to finish my 4 year degree. Graduate school opened up the door to study abroad bringing my total up to 9 schools on 3 continents, so I'm kind of a university expert. Somehow, even though George Fox is a private university that functions squarely in public space, the hash tag is a reality.

As you move in intimate, personal, social (we'll get to that, but it's 4 feet - 12 feet), and public space (when people are more than 12 feet from each other) how can make #BeKnow a reality?

P.S. Dunbar noticed a tipping point[95] happens in public space, or around 150 people. Under 150 people we can *yada* everyone, over 150 and the best we can do is *d'ath* (know about) people.

Humans can only recognize around 1,500 people and have 500 acquaintances, but Tribe, where we can know and be known, is capped at 150. Far too often success seems to live beyond this number (that's why we defined success early on).

idea 3

IT STARTS
WITH ME

"Who you share what with when" is the best definition of curate I've heard.

There is a muddle, but also an alliteration.

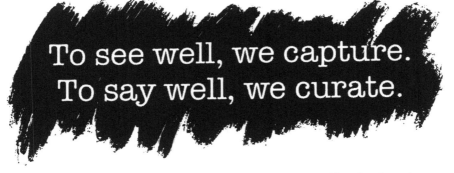

To see well, we capture.
To say well, we curate.

Back in **SUCCESS** (Idea Five), we talked about Jesus' 12 disciples making disciples (72), who made disciples — putting the total number of disciples, grand-disciples and great-grand-disciples over 500. One of the reasons this Jesus message spread so well is it was highly curated.

Jesus curated what he said. He told stories to the crowd (public space) and explained them to the 12 (personal space / super-family). He told his disciples to curate, when he said make disciples in Jerusalem, Judea, Samaria, and to the ends of the earth.[96]

188

Fisterra, Spain (*finis* is Latin for end, and where we get finish, *terrae* means land or earth. It's where we get terrain) is a three day walk from Santiago, not much for the 200,000 people who walk 500 miles to Santiago each year. Locals call it the Camino, or Camino de Santiago. If it sounds familiar, Hemingway mentioned it in *The Sun Also Rises,* but Hemingway isn't why people walk it.

Spain wasn't what Jesus was talking about, when he said the ends of the earth, but when you stand in Fisterra, it feels like you are there. It's the same in San Diego, there is no land to be seen, but somewhere the blue from the water melds into the blue in the sky.

When James, started a church in Santiago, in some way, curation was done. He'd reached the ends of the earth.

Jerusalem was where the disciples were. They didn't have to go anywhere, because they were in Jerusalem. It's also where people were like them. They ate the same foods, danced to the same songs, and laughed at the same jokes.

Where is your Jerusalem — where are you day in, and day out, where people are like you?

Hopefully there is huge overlap between kin / super-family and your Jerusalem. This is why *work family* language has emerged.

To curate well, which is to say well, you always start in Jerusalem.

Judea took some travel, but culturally people were the same. Samaria was about the same distance as Judea, but when you traveled north instead of south, the culture changed. To get to Fisterra (59 hours by car, but no one had cars 2,000 years ago) all kinds of geographic and cultural distance had to be crossed.

Start in Jerusalem, then Judea, then Samaria, then Fisterra. Who you share what with when matters, and should start where you are, where people are like you.

Notice I said where people are like you, not where people like you. Curation needs commonality, at least in the begining, not an echo chamber.

Long before you see the *Night is Electric* frontman buried up to his neck in sand, the words, "it starts with me — a meditation," silently appear on the screen. Honestly, its best to jump on YouTube, watch the *Start a War* video,[97] then come back to reading.

When Van Meter sings,

> Went down, thinking I could change,
> bring it all back to life.
> Now I see the battles in me,
> gotta bring it from the inside out

even the music senses the game has changed.

Famous people are often miserable because they curated backwards. Social media makes it easier than ever to conquer public space while ignoring intimate space. We think we are at war with the world, when often we are at war with ourselves.

It's easy to confuse success with a stage, but unless it starts with me, it's fruitless. To be overly clear that means not *tov*.

190

Who is always where I am?

Me.

Curation should start with me, because

98

Who is like me? Well, it doesn't get more like me than me. To put it in Edward Hall's proxemics terminology, intimate space always includes me. After all, I'm always within 18 inches of myself.

So what are you saying to you?

It's a muddle, sometimes we've got to see what we say, so we can say something different, something more true. Set your phone to sound an alarm at a random time. When it sounds, stop and finish the sentence: The story I'm telling myself[99] is....

Be warned: I lifted that question from Brené Browns Netflix special and it's a game changer. Like most stuff from Brené, this question is a call to bravery.

Do you remember your reaction when you read you were an artist, back in **SEE**? This isn't just sketches and sonnets. Everyone I've met is an amazing storyteller too.

People have walked into my office for years telling me the most creative stories about all the tragic things that could happen. They may be negative, but they are still creative.

When a Dad catches his son sneaking something behind the garage with his buddies and ends up in my office, the kid is scared. Dad is riddled with shame, but it took a while to see that. Time after time the story Dad is telling himself is he's a bad Father and his son's life is heading down the toilet.

What is a different story Dad could be telling himself, about himself?

What could he be telling his son?

Notice I didn't say what the kid was sneaking. It doesn't matter: a beer, a cigarette, a peek at a playboy. None of these things should be minimized. Unless the kid is 18, all of these things are illegal, but that's not the point... what they are saying is.

193

Grown men, when asked what they snuck behind their dad's garage all have a story. Time after time, the dads that are most angry have a story they haven't shared. One recounted years of infidelity he traced back to the lust the playboy stirred up. Another wept remembering the friend he snuck schnapps with is dead because he drove.

What looked like anger, was fear and shame. Anger is a secondary emotion and there is always something underneath it. Time after time, as Dad bravely told his story to his son, everything changed. But, it started with Dad owning the story he was telling himself.

Sometimes we need to write it out first, (here's some space):

Intimate space is such a small number because those people can help us see differently. He wasn't a bad dad, in fact he was a really good one, he just needed someone else to speak those words into existence, so he could see them. The son, wasn't a bad kid and hadn't ruined his life. He had made a decision that could have huge consequences. Someone had to speak that reality, so he could see it too.

It starts with me, then it flows to we — from intimate space (kin), onward to personal (super-family), then to lucky 13. Before we get there, we need to remember what we learned on the playground: no take-backs.

idea FOUR
NO TAKE-BACKS

When I turned eight, my birthday party was a sleep over. Marshall lived in the double-wide across the street, so his dad walked him over to our trailer. Dropping him off, he asked my mom out on their first date, a concert.

Before they got married, Dad took a job at a ranch on the other side of Colorado. Since they had a long distance relationship, Marshall and I spent hours in the covered bed of a burgundy GM truck. As they drove across Colorado, we played and traded GI Joes.

Mom and Dad had one rule: no take-backs. If I offered Hawk, Scarlett, and Sgt. Stalker for Snake Eyes, and Marshall took the trade, it was done. No take-backs, period. For the record, Marshall would never trade Snake Eyes.

No take-backs was a rule. We agreed on it, and our parents enforced it. That's how it is with trades. When it comes to SAY, there is no external rule, no-take backs just is. Once something is said it can't be unsaid, no matter how much someone may want to.

Tov is about multiplication, not mediocrity of morality, but God didn't say, "be fruitful and multiply." At least not to people. People were told, "replenish the earth and subdue it."[100] We are supposed to organize things in such a way that everything, from anchovies to zebras, can find and live *tov*.

God said it, and even God plays by the no take-back rule.

196

2016 Nobel Prize for Literature winner Bob Dylan penned these lyrics:

> He saw an animal up on a hill
> chewing up so much grass until it was filled.
> He saw milk coming out
>   but he didn't know how
> Ah, think I'll call it a cow[101]

Dylan has equally compelling verses about a bear, bull, pig, sheep, and what I guess is a snake. (You'll have to listen to the song and decide yourself.). Bob Dylan, whose birth name is Robert Zimmerman, understood naming is part of "replenish and subdue." He embraced the no-take back rule.

Counselors make a good living on the no take-back rule. Hurtful things said in the moment leave deep scars, that's the *Ra* side of performative utterance.

When it comes to living *tov;*

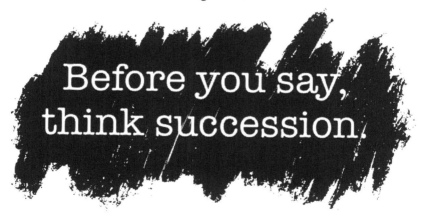

Even today, when our words create worlds (that's being fruitful and multiplying), we are charged to organize them - no take-backs. Sabbatical can be really helpful here, we'll get specific in SUCCESSION, but I needed to plant the seed now. Who you say what to when, might be the most important factor in long term success.

NAPKIN SCRIBBLES

Even though I'm never more than a few feet from a notebook, I love writing on bar napkins. Some things need to be thought, crumpled up, and thrown away.

> Sometimes it is necessary to go a long distance out of the way in order to come back a short distance correctly.
>
> — Edward Albee, The Zoo Story

I'm an idea guy. Some ideas are stepping stones. We can't get us from one point to the next without them. Other ideas need to be said because they are blocking the way. We need to clear the surface, so other ideas can get oxygen.

For years, this stressed Tricia out. I have zero construction experience, but she thought I was going to knock walls out of our house — because that's what I said. Our phrase became, "napkin scribble." When I said it, she knew she was safe and I was just exploring.

When Christa, the Director of Operations I'd worked with for years, overheard me say "napkin scribble" to Tricia, I found out she always wondered what to plan for and when I was dreaming. If you are an external processor find a phrase because there are no take-backs.

What is your napkin scribbles phrase?

Who needs to know it?

Simple phrases like, "napkin scribble," create worlds and organize them in a way that keeps *Ra* at bay.

It doesn't matter if you are in intimate space, personal space, social space, or public space — kin, super-family, tribe, acquaintances, or merely people you recognize... if you want to live *tov* you've got to:

see,   say,   and separate together. When you do, these people become your team.

You might want to work through the previous sections with your team, but here are some questions to get you started.

Where do you and your team agree on "what is?"

Where do you differ?

Doing a **S.W.O.T.** (**S**trength, **W**eakness, **O**ppurtunity, and **T**hreat) analysis[102] is a great way to check a teams' alignment.

Use post it notes and give everybody a chance to share what they believe the **S**trengths and **W**eaknesses of a team or project are. You'll quickly get an idea of how closely the "what is" of your group align.

Sharing **O**pportunities and **T**hreats are an easy way to get at "what can be?" What alignment does your team have on what can be?

Where are you not seeing the same thing?

There are no take-backs, but there are do-overs. Knowing your team inhabits different worlds might mean you need to create a common one. Fortunatly, you already know how. Remember words create worlds. Don't take it lightly, but speak some into existance. Saying "napkin scribbles" did just that.

201

P.S. Going through **SEE** with your team isn't just helpful, it's often needed. Do you all agree on what **SUCCESS** is? If you don't define the win, you will lose.

You don't have to go at it alone. Coaching (www.FindYourTov.com) can help flesh out questions and get to where you're going.

P.P.S. If it becomes clear, when you SAY together, that you don't SEE together, your first response should be "SABBATH together."[103].

idea 5
CLARITY NOT VOLUME

In his in-laws kitchen, you'd never know Jamie was a West Point grad, or highly decorated officer in the military. The best never flaunt it, but when Jamie said,

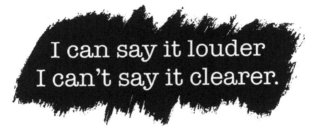

I can say it louder
I can't say it clearer.

the fact he'd led troops and bases alike was evident.

I would have added, "Do you need me to say it louder?" He didn't have to. Jamie mastered clarity, 10 words is all it took. When it comes to say, clarity is king, and brevity his cousin.

Confidence and courage are common topics, but you don't get there without clarity.[104]

clarity → confidence → courage

is etched in notebooks, and has been wiped off of countless dry erase boards.

Courage, is confidence under pressure:
  No more.
  No less.

Very little, if anything, can be done to lower pressure, when it's there it's there. The only way to ensure courage is gain confidence.

Confidence rises and falls on clarity. If you are confident (not cocky, or crazy, but confident) you have clarity. When someone lacks confidence, you can bet the bank, they lack clarity.

Where in your life could you gain confidence by getting clarity?

Often, "how" matters as much as "what."
How have you gained clarity in the past?

Unfortunately, saying things louder never makes them clearer. Lean in close, look me in the eye and you can whisper. If you understand what you're saying, I probably will too. (Whispering is always easier in intimate space.)

205

Where are you attempting to substitute volume
for clarity?

Yelling isn't the only way to be louder. If the
conditions are right, a voice can carry almost
600 feet, that's two football fields — well over,
what Edward Hall called public space.

More than 110 kilometers (69 miles) separate the
two airports in Frankfurt Germany. Ben, Adam,
and I didn't realize there were two airports:
HHN (Frankfurt-Hahn) where our flight to Latvia,
booked separately on a different airline, departed
from, and FRA (Frankfurt) where our flight from
Chicago had just landed.

Our jet lagged voices got very loud, very quickly.
We didn't increase our decibel level, but reached
in our pocket and posted.

Deb, in New Haven, Indiana (4,270 miles away
from us) added, "@Heather" and her daughter
in Stuttgart (204 kilometers from us — I'm
switching to kilometers because these places
don't even use the same measurements) replied.
Separated by six time zones, we were silently
shouting for the world to hear.

With historically unprecedented amplification in
each of our pockets to say in public space to
more than the 1,500 people we might be able
to recognize is easy. How often do we confuse
volume with clarity? Add in the dopamine hit[105]
we get with a like and volume can even serve as
a substitute for success.

The irony is public relationships aren't really a thing, at least not in themselves. Public relationships are a collection of social relationships, which are a collection of personal relationships, which are a collection of intimate relationships.

Social Space, is how people act when they are 4-8 feet from each other. This is why, when COVID-19 hit, people adopted the phrase, "social distancing." Like third-wheel gives us a hint, we shifted from intimate to personal space, 13 being an unlucky number has everything to do with the shift from personal to social space. Think back to a personal space gathering you were part of and draw the relationships between those 3-12 people.

With three people, there are three potential intimate relationships, one you aren't part of. Add one more person and there are three relationships you are part of, but three more you aren't. At four, there are more potential intimate relationships you aren't part of (6), than you could be part of (4). For every person you add, you have one more intimate relationship. The relationships you aren't part of grows exponentially. When you have a group of 12 there are 66 potential intimate relationships you can't be part of. The bigger the group the easier it is to substitute volume for clarity.

People want to be heard and seen.

If you tried to do the same map with social space (13-150 people) it would be very difficult, if not impossible. Intimate relationships looked like a line, and personal space a triangle. Social space is stacking personal space triangles.

INTIMATE   PERSONAL   SOCIAL

There will be intimate relationships that connect personal relationships in interesting ways, but in the end, social space is all about personal relationships connected by intimate relationships. Try to map a group (I'd stick with personal space, because this page is small).

If your map looked like an organizational chart, it probably wasn't very accurate. Org charts are an attempt to sketch out social and public space. The problem is they are based on positions, not people. *Ra* often creeps in here. We can cultivate intimate relationships, but they can't be manufactured. Even in intimate relationships, one person brings clarity another never could.

Some things don't need to get louder. Staying in intimate, or personal space can be the most *tov* thing. If you've got to get bigger, going 3D helps.

Legos are my favorite to attempt a 3D social space map. Not only does 3D help us play, it reminds us that *tov* doesn't always look the same way. In fact it rarely does.

I'm gonna pick up the pieces and build a Lego house. When things go wrong we can knock it down.

- Ed Sheeran

Playing this way also illuminates capacity, an essential ingredient in clarity. Google image search Lego, and you'll see the 4x2 block is iconic. This means, at the very most eight blocks can attach on top and eight on bottom. There are some long thin blocks, but since the most common blocks are 4x2 its more likely to have between four and six on top and the same on bottom.

Another game, telephone, shows us how clarity can be lost.

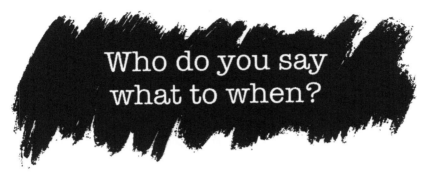

Who do you say what to when?

In general, SAY works best when we are connected with people. It's not just that say works best when intimate space overflows to personal space, which overflows to social space and that overflows to public space. Things are adopted along those same lines.

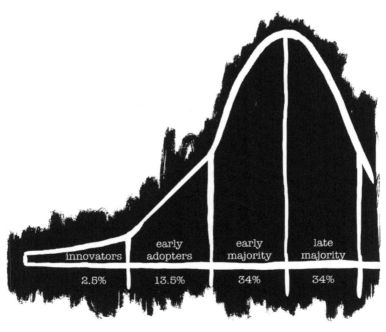

innovators	early adopters	early majority	late majority
2.5%	13.5%	34%	34%

The last 16% are called laggards, they may never adopt something new or get the message, so I leave them out of the equation.

In your tribe of 150, only about 4 people (2.5%) need to hear and understand something new at first. Those 4 will each share it with about 5 people each (13.5%). If those people agree, they will only share it with a couple people each, but that will put you over the chasm and into an early majority. Once you are over the chasm, change is inevitable.

What becomes apparent is that while you can do anything, you can't do everything, so stuff needs to be separated.

MOVEMENT VI
SEPARATE

idea ONE
WHAT WILL BE?

Henry Ford is the reason you've got a car in your garage. He said, "If I asked people what they wanted, they would have said faster horses."

Bill Gates may be the reason you've got a computer on your desk, but Steve Jobs is the reason we carry them in our pockets. Jobs quoted Henry Ford, and got a bit more candid:

> People don't know what they want until you show them... our task is to read things that aren't on the page yet.
> - Steve Jobs

[107]

Sounds like Steve had learned to see.

Living in a *tov* and *Ra* world means *Ra* will find ways to creep in. Doing the same thing and expecting different results isn't just one way to define insanity, it's also a tell-tale sign of *Ra*, or as Ford said,

> If you always do what you've always done you'll always get what you've always got."

On the off chance, you are at a friends' house and this book was on the coffee table and you randomly opened to this page, please go back to the beginning. At least, start in SEE. It's always better to answer the question, "What is?" (page

214

93–98) and explore, "What can be?" (page 110–117) before deciding, "What will be?"

Without *what can be,* *what will be* becomes monotony and mediocrity. More of the same might be multiplication, but it's not the same as *tov.*

Former Disney Imagineer, McNair Wilson, takes all the ideas *what can be* generated and declares, *"It's a Menu, Not a Ballot!."*[108]

Now, after seeing and saying, it's finally time to separate.

Last millennium, McNair had a three step process for separating:

> pick,
> package,
> promote.

In his book *Hatch!* the words changed.

> grab replaced pick,
> group, replaced package
> grow, replaced promote,

but the process stayed the same. The choice is yours:

> grab or pick,
> group or package,
> grow or promote.

mix and match the g's and p's if you'd like, but do it.

STEP ONE: GRAB (or PICK)[109]

Don't vote, just pick something. If you are doing this with a team and the *what can be* that most captivates you doesn't get picked, after grow, go back and pick it. Have the team run the process again. (You might actually have multiple teams with multiple *tov's* in the same room. An herb makes dinner yummy, but a basil garden gets boring fast.)

When you look at all the things that can be, all the things you came up with in **SEE** (pages 110–117), what catches your attention, maybe even captivates you?

(Write it in the center of the next page).

It doesn't matter which ideas we DO NOT like. What matters is selecting the idea that works best.

- McNair

110

STEP TWO: GROUP (or PACKAGE)[111]

People who knew me well said,

"So, is this _____ 2.0,"

when I told them I was starting *Brother Dog* (The non-profit coaching company that helps people process "Find Your Tov" and make the impact they were made for. Half a dozen dreams filled in the blank. Ideas like *Brother Dog* and *Finding Tov* had been circulating in my mind and soul for decades.

Look back at your list of *what can be*. If there are adjacent ideas, group them with the thing that captured your attention. Write them around the one thing on the previous page. Play with this. Have fun, use a different color, or attempt a different font — if you've got to package, it might as well be a pretty package.

STEP THREE: GROW (or PROMOTE)[112]

Play with the idea for a little bit. Looking just at that idea; ask, *what it can be*. Imagine how it could grow if ended for a season.

Where could it be in a year?

How about in six years, or seven?

I know it was a menu, not a ballot, but we've been trained to vote and rank. Even though Warren Buffet said, "I can't recall making a list in my life,"[113] the 25/5 rule still works. Look at your list of things that can be. Put the top 25 in order from what you want to achieve the most, to what you want to achieve the least. The thing, or things, you picked should be on the top of the list.

1. _____

2. _____

3. _____

4. _____

5. _____

6. _____   7. _____

8. _____   9. _____

10. _____   11. _____

12. _____   13. _____

14. _____   15. _____

16. _____   17. _____

18. _____   19. _____

20. _____   21. _____

22. _____   23. _____

24. _____   25. _____

Now, draw a line between 5 and 6. If you are ADD like me, or trust the research that having 2-3 goals means you'll accomplish 2-3 and when you bump to 4-10 goals you'll only hit 1-2,[114] then draw the line between 3 and 4, or 2 and 3.

Above the line you've got your to-do list, below the line is an avoid at all costs list. Things that are really close to your *tov*, maybe 2 or 3 degrees off, can be the most *Ra* to living *miyn tov*.

Another way to help focus (not fixate, but focus). Is to ask, "What am I doing that's important?"

Often people confuse what is important and what is urgent, so make a list of the urgent thing you are doing too.

Maybe its easier to organize them like this; it's
called the Eisenhower Matrix

URGENT   NOT
                URGENT

I
M
P
O
R
T
A
N
T

N
O
T

I
M
P
O
R
T
A
N
T

DO the things that are important and urgent.

PLAN the things that are important, but not urgent.

DELEGATE the things that are urgent, but not important. There is a good chance, if it's not important to you, it's not your *miyn tov*, but it probably is *min tov* for someone else. Helping someone else live their *tov* is the difference between dumping and delegating.

ELIMINATE what's neither important nor urgent.

Remember, when we say yes to something, we need to say no to hundreds of other things. So, if you're not saying an enthusiastic "YES!" say a simple, but certain "No."

(Remember Derek Silvers quote back on page 78)

idea TWO
CHIP DAVID

I bumped into David once — literally, bumped into Michelangelo's David.

Jenny had connected me with a friend in Copenhagen who was hosting me on a layover day. Back in 1913, Edvard Eriksen, a Danish sculpture made a bronze statue called *Den Lille Havfrue*. We were going to see it. Since it was raining, we cut through alleys covered with awnings, darting from shop to shop. Turning the corner to Lageline Promenade, while trying to have a conversation with the person behind me, and my forehead was the first part of me to notice the 17 foot tall sculpture, with a thunk.

Something was lost in translation. I thought my host was saying it was the original David, turns out it was a bronze cast. Google filled me in on the details, as it turns out there are two copies in Florence alone.

When Michelangelo was asked how he made such an amazing sculpture, at least according to Michelangelo Buonarroti, he said,

> The sculpture is already complete within the marble block, before I start my work. It's already there, I just have to chisel away the superfluous material."[115]

To put it a bit more apocryphally (and poetically),

You just chip away the stone that doesn't look like David.
- Michelangelo

Until that moment, for me, a negative vibe surrounded chipping away. Separate was what my parents did before the divorce. When you think of separate what thoughts fill your head?

Michelangelo is a ninja. We're still talking about the renaissance sculpture, not the nunchaku wielding, orange mask wearing, teenage turtle. The artist could move from SEE and SEPARATE without stutter or stumble. (Since his was commission work, SAY had to be in there too.)

To separate, weather chipping away or cutting off, isn't necessarily negative. Jesus took pause, and reminded people pruning (or being pruned) is a step to *tov,* not a punishment.[117] Even back then, people defaulted to dichotomies, confusing categories for *tov.* If something was pruned, it must not have been good.

If marble was the metaphor, Jesus would have said "chip," but he went more organic talking about plants and pruning. If you struggle to separate, don't underestimate the power of metaphor. Language creates culture, words create worlds, so how can you talk about separate in a positively charged way?

Back in the creation poem, plants were the clearest example of *tov* — remember the redundancies, fruit with seed in it.

> I am[118] the true vine, and my Father is the gardener. He cuts off every branch in me that bears no fruit, while every branch that does bear fruit he prunes so that it will be even more fruitful.[119]

Fruit is the focus of what Jesus said. It's all about *tov*.

Thousands of years later, the steps are the same. You can't get fruit without pruning — see, say, then do the work and separate.

In Greek, the root word is *aire* (ΑΙΡΕΙ). Branches that aren't fruitful are *aire* — cut off. This is where is gets real. To live *tov* means cutting off things that aren't fruitful. Writing more about this, is probably procrastination and right now is the time to prune.

What in your life isn't fruitful?

Before you go cutting something off because it isn't fruitful, remember fruit is seasonal. Don't take an axe out in the winter because nothing bears fruit in the winter.

Back in *Not Now* (pages 64–74) we talked about timelines. Before you *aire,* because something isn't fruitful, make sure you give it time.

The statue we were walking to, when I bumped into David, was made in 1913, the fruit of a fairy tale written 76 years earlier by Hans Christian Anderson. *Den Lille Havfrue* was the Danish name of the statue and the fairy tale. It translates to *The Little Mermaid.* Disney added flair to fruit, music and animation, 150 years later.

Fruit sometimes takes 76 years, another fruit might take 150, so

Check before you chop.

Don't underestimate benign neglect. Some will be eager to *aire,* others fearful, and all most everyone will need to mourn.

Sometimes separate means stepping away from a job. That has real world implications, spaghetti number stuff. It could mean cutting out a toxic relationship. For that reason, *Brother Dog* started with two mental health professionals on its Board of Directors. If *Brother Dog* stepped into that arena, it would be *Ra,* so we don't. It's not *tov* to be alone, so we partner with mental health professionals. Often "check before you chop" means talking to someone.

Things that aren't fruitful get *aire*, but things that are fruitful get *kath-aire* (ΚΑΘΑΊΡΕΙ). Adding *kath* changes the tool from a chainsaw to a chisel. Pruning is precise, but it's still cutting off. The takeaway here is

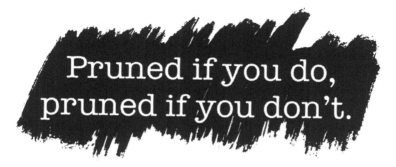

Pruned if you do, pruned if you don't.

What are areas in your life that need some pruning?

One of Herod the Great's palaces is next to a green house, on a little family farm. It hasn't been excavated, but Bob knows where it is.

I didn't dig it. Blaming that on the partial excavation would be easy, and a great pun, but Tsh Oxenreider noted,

When everything is awesome, nothing is awesome.

- Tsh Oxenreider

My first trip to Israel was awesome. By that point in the trip, too much awesome had happened too quickly, so I walked through that families field. I needed normal, even awesome needs to be pruned sometimes.

Wine came from these grapes, but it wasn't the season for fruit. They'd pruned the grapevines.

Grapes are harvested, then branches are pruned back to the vine, that way energy is conserved during the winter. A little nub is on the vine where the branch used to be, and where it will be again. For now, it's just a nub. The farmer told me this was abiding. Abide is a sabbath word, and it has to happen after pruning.

How are you planning to abide after you prune?
(You will need the sabbath.)

Maybe the muddle is see (sabbath), say, separate
(sabbath). Then again it could be (sabbath) see,
say, (sabbath) separate. All I know is, it's a
muddle.

idea 3

ALMONDS &
ORBITS

Nothing is *tov* on the second day. This is a big deal. Day One[121] tells us the way *tov* comes to be (see, say, separate). The third day[122] has two *tovs*, painting a picture of multiplication, but *tov* is conspicuously absent on the second day.

Poets count words and syllables. When they do the multiplication comes into fuller focus.

Hyphenated words (על-פני) count for two both times. Rules are flexible and bending them is part of the art. Eminem can rhyme orange with: four inch, door hinge, storage, porridge, and George.[123] There is wiggle room. How many of Shakespeare's sonnets stretch a one syllable word to two?

Genesis opens with seven words in the first line

בראשית ברא אלהים את
השמים ואת הארץ:

then fourteen in the second

והארץ היתה תהו ובהו וחשך
על-פני תהום ורוח אלהים
מרהפת על-פני המים:

232

Count numbers and this poem is about multiplication. *Tov* is multiplication. This is underscored by the fact it shows up seven times too (twice on the third and sixth day). On the second day, where is *tov*?

In the same way, pointing out to Adam that he wasn't *tov* alone, helps us understand the nature of *tov*. Missing from the second day tells us something about *tov* too.

The second day[124] was dedicated to dividing. Water was seperated from water...that's it.

Division,
by itself,
isn't tov.

When the light was pulled out of the darkness, each got a name. Day and night danced. That's what things are divided to do. Divided and dancing is *tov*.

Separating creative and critical, like we did back on page 111 (*What Can Be?*), is even more difficult when our default is anything but divided to dance. Lining creatives up on the left wall and critical thinkers on the right is reminiscent of a Junior High dance, nobody has fun. Deep down, when we are not dancing, we know something is missing.

We long for more.

In your world, what's divided that you long to see dance?

How about divided things you can't imagine dancing?

It's been a few pages, but back in ORIGIN STORY (p. 23) we learned the Italian word for almond is mandorla. The labyrinth from the floor of Chartes Cathedral is tattooed on my right forearm. To get to it you've got to walk through a door with this above it.

Do you see the mandorla?

125

If you can't envision the overlapping circles, draw them in. If it were a Venn diagram one circle is labeled "God" and the other "man." Jesus is both. That's the point of the mandorla above the door. To stay an almond, there are God places, Jesus doesn't go. Jesus said, "the Father and I are one,"126 and he owned, "no one knows the day or the hour, not even the angles in heaven, not the Son, but only the Father."127

This isn't a tight rope walk. There is tension, rather a mandorla has flow. Orbit may be the best way to describe it.

Gordon MacKenzie wrote *Orbiting the Giant Hairball* after he retired from Hallmark. A hairball is what happens when stagnation substitutes for stillness.

He imagined how Hallmark started. Mr. Hall thinking to himself...

> "My gut tells me it would be most effective if I did it this way. And it would make sense to do it that way." *This* and *that* Hall's first two business decisions were also the first two hairs of a hairball.[128]

> There was a time when there was no hairball....two hairs unite. Then they are joined by another. And another. And another. Before long, where there once was nothing, this impenetrable mass has begun to form.[129]

A hairball, as he's describing it, is a motionless mandorala. Sure, we have to draw them that way, but what we've captured isn't complete. Like division, policies and procedures, rules and regulations, have a necessary place, but have you noticed,

> every new policy is another hair for the hairball. Hairs are never taken away, only added. Even frequent reorganizations have failed to remove hairs (people, sometimes; hairs, never).[130]

Hairball, in and of themselves aren't a problem unless they are unexamined. What are some of the hairs that make up your hairball?

Chances are good some of these are some of these sacred cows that would make better steaks. Which ones do you think should go on the grill?

We need to learn to SAY these things to our team. Church folk are comfortable with page 164 "What was your favorite toy growing up?" questions. What would happen if you ask others on your team what hairs they see, but don't understand? Chances are good there's already division. This is a chance to dance.

Sharing the story of how the hairball came to be, is often invigorating. It avoids entanglement and often helps launch orbits. MacKenzie explains:

> Many a Hallmarker succumb to the pull of this relentless gravity. They are the ones who, suspended in the grey sameness of the bowels of the institution wonder "what year is it."

> Others, in their attmepts to avoid the threatened limbo of the Hairball, escape to other endeavors — often, ironically, to other Hairballs.

> Then there are those few...who manage to actively engage the oppurtunities Hallmark presents without being sucked into the Hairball of Hallmark. This is accomplished by orbiting.[131]

What is orbiting your hairball?
If it's nothing what could (or even should) be?

What is your hairball orbiting?

To be of optimum value to the corporate endeavor, you must invest enough individuality to counteract the pull of Corporate Gravity, but not so much that you escape that pull altogether.[132]

Is there something you've seen (and said) that needs to be separated and launched into orbit?

idea FOUR
ALOHA

Faith Lutheran Church required ushers to wear navy blue blazers. Jim Noll put his on over an aloha shirt, wore flip-flops and board shorts. In 1958, the summer after Waimea Bay, he went to Hawaii with his brother Greg "da Bull" and hung out with Duke Kahanamoku, the Big Kahuna, himself. Board shorts & Aloha shirts had been Jim's uniform ever since.

I'd never surfed and if you are not a surfer, these names and places mean nothing. I was in California to learn to be a pastor. I didn't realize these were surf legends (although, if Jim heard that he would say he wasn't). To me, a guy named Jim, just asked if I wanted to come on an adventure.

Somewhere at Swami's, I realized surf lessons from someone in their 60's should be a required course for anyone training to be a pastor, but that's a book in itself. After my internship, I moved back to Indiana. Jim sent me with the same Aloha, he'd greeted me with.

Aloha cultures, ones that send and receive with the same phrase, understand and embrace orbit.

Chipping away at the idea of Aloha, "I don't know why you say goodbye, I say hello" got stuck in my head. John Lennon said it was three minutes of contradiction and meaningless juxtaposition.[133] The song is full of opposites, but not contradiction. For every yes, there must be a thousand no's — these things are divided to dance.

241

Orbit embracing Aloha-languages celebrate separate. We're talking about *ciao* in Italy, and *chào* in Vietnam. Hello and Goodbye are *cześć* in Polish. Nothing points to orbit more clearly than the use of *vanakkam* in the Indian language Tamil. It is a version of the word, "come." Vanakkam means, "welcome" as a greeting, and "I will come again," when leaving.[134]

Sometimes it's stuff, other times people, but everything that's pruned has a way of coming back around. No matter when or why you are separating, orbit infers depart and return are part of the dance. We better learn to do them well.

Like drawing or poetry, thinking like an anthropologist helps us see. If you, or your tribe, were being studied, what would they say your welcome rituals were?

How I greet my wife when we wake up in the morning matters. When I've been on the road for weeks or months, it's different and should be. How do you greet (or want to greet) differently when it's been a while?

Thinking through this is key to not burning up on reentry.

Greeting is different than meeting. It assumes an orbit, that what you are greeting has been met and sent. *Shalom* means peace in Hebrew; it's used as a greeting for receiving and sending blessing. The Arabic word *salaam* means and does the same. Built into these words, is that things are sent with a blessing.

What are your sending rituals?
If you don't have any, what could they be?

Disney insiders call the fireworks a goodnight kiss. Walt knew the power of sending well. He embraced orbit with his sending ritual. He didn't say goodbye, but "see you real soon."

In the military, knowing you'll be gone a little longer, drill sergeants give paper and pens to the soldiers and they write letters to loved ones.

Pruning people for an evening, or season, means adjusting and adapting. At times knowing you'll orbit brings assurance, other times dread.

We can embrace both.

Hurt people, hurt people.

At church, chances are good that early on in the service you were asked to stand and greet those around you. Growing up this was called, "passing the peace."

Church used to start with a time of confession, before people entered the worship space. Early on, this time wasn't exclusively for admitting you've done something wrong to God, but also to say sorry to the people you'd hurt. Admitting wrong, and hearing the wrong released, is a reentry ritual we need to recover.

Are there people you've wronged? What would a daily reentry ritual look like? When you LOOK BACK ask yourself, "Have I wronged anyone this week?" Embrace a reentry ritual, send a text and apologize. If you need to talk face to face, schedule it first thing Monday morning.

I'm not leaving space to jot names of people you need to text, just pick up the phone and do it.

Divided to dance is different than divided by hurt.

Orbits are healthy, but some unnecessarily elongate without reentry rituals. Jim adopted Aloha, what can you do to remind yourself you are in orbit with everyone you meet?

Starting with admitting something has changed embraces Aloha.

P.S. Orbiting people is one thing, owning we orbit sin is another. Church people call it sin. My non-religious friends are more comfortable with bad habits. Friends in recovery (some of my favorite people, by the way) claim the name addiction. The Hebrew Scriptures, at least the King James translation, call it iniquity.

Ezekiel is a prophet who said

> the Son shall not bear the iniquity of the father,[136]

but Deuteronomy says God will

> visit the iniquity of the father upon their children unto the third and fourth generation.[137]

In the final movement, **SUCCESSION**, we'll do a deep dive into the this, but a counselor said it best. Tricia and I went to him for marriage counseling. At the end of the intake session he refused to take us on as clients. He said, "you don't have marriage issues" then looked at me, and only me, square in the eyes and continued, "you need to deal with your shit or your shit will deal with you." It's the only time he ever swore, but he needed to, so I would listen. Over the next months and years we started chipping away at issues, but to this day they orbit.

How to avoid sin, adjust habits, or break addictions is an essential conversation that I'll leave to more qualified people. Remember, "not bear," is a **SEPARATE** concept. Kids don't have to carry their parents junk. At the same time, they do need to deal with it.

Visit is an orbit word. Al-Anon, a group for friends and family of problem drinkers, exemplifies this. Recognizing iniquity orbits is essential. In the end, it helps us understand orbit.

247

idea FIVE
IT AIN'T EASY

Don't confuse simple with easy.

See,   Say,   Separate,
is simple, but don't say three easy steps.

It wasn't easy to see, it took practice,
persistence, and learning to Sabbath. If anything
should be easy, it's Sabbath...unfortunately it
wasn't either. It never is.

My first year as a Pastor, I committed to taking
the first Tuesday of every month, driving to
Camp Lutherhaven and using their Day Away
Room. I knew if I was going to lead a Church,
I needed to see, so I carved these days out
months before I even started the job.

On Monday, the day before my first Day Away,
our Chairman's son went missing. He'd left a
cryptic note for his wife. Fortunatly, we were
able to trace credit card charges to a hotel in
Detroit where he attempted suicide.

I spent Monday with the family and arranged a Pastor in Detroit to visit the ICU. The next day, I felt shame even thinking about taking that day away. There was nothing else I could do.

Sabbath is simple, but don't think it's easy. *Ra* will fight tooth and nail, even if it's through an unseen thing like shame.

Say is easy, as long as we aren't worried about *tov* turning to *Ra*. Even superstar rhetoricians (aka say-ers) like Alexander Hamilton, admit

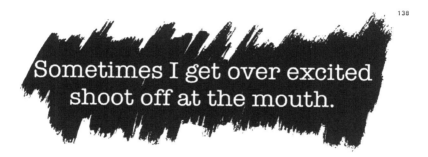

Sometimes I get over excited shoot off at the mouth.

(at least according to Lin-Manuel Miranda). To live *tov*, say is hard too. If see and say are difficult, we should expect the same from separate.

Bob Goff starts each chapter of *Love Does* with "I used to ... but now I know ..." When it comes to finding and living your *tov* as an individual or organization it's a great template. Fill in the blanks:

I used to _____

_____

_____

,

but now I _____

_____

_____.

Maybe you've realized more than one

I used to _____

_____

_____

,

but now I _____

_____

_____.

People often say, "When God closes a door, he opens a window." Something about that never sat right with me, it's easier than my experiences ever have been. I don't know if God is even in the business of opening and closing doors. I do know, when Batman closes a door, someone goes out a window."

Out of the thirty-one chapters, Bob opened one up with

139

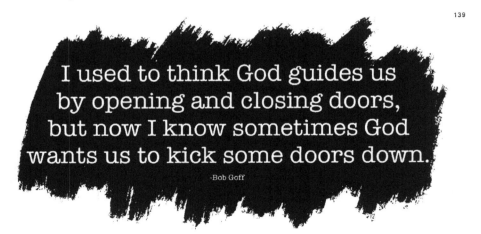

I used to think God guides us by opening and closing doors, but now I know sometimes God wants us to kick some doors down.
-Bob Goff

What are some doors you know need to be kicked in?

Neil Gaiman, author and Amanda Palmer's[140] husband, misquoted G.K. Chesterton when he wrote

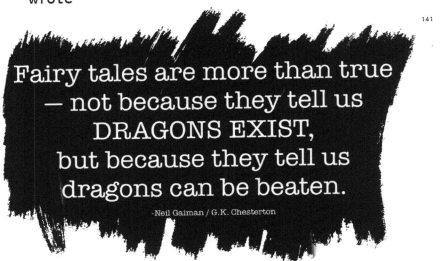

Fairy tales are more than true — not because they tell us DRAGONS EXIST, but because they tell us dragons can be beaten.

-Neil Gaiman / G.K. Chesterton

When Gaiman realized he misquoted Chesterton he said, "I'm perfectly happy for anyone to attribute it to either of us. The sentiment is his, the phrasing is mine." It doesn't matter who said it, it's true.

God isn't a doorman. If God was, I'd have to wonder if closing doors is mainly to let us know they can be kicked in.

Nowadays, Matt is the Executive Director of an organization that realizes Pastors aren't counselors. Cross Connections separated from the church, but orbit on a way that makes mental health a priority, normalizing professional counseling and making it accessible. The organization (Cross Connections) and the individual (Matt) are living *tov*.

Matt knows a thing or two about kicking in doors. Before he was an executive director, Matt was Seabee. *Construimus Batuimus,* latin for "We build, We fight," is the official motto, but I had to google that. The unofficial motto that Matt taught me was, "Embrace the suck."

Even knowing we will orbit, there is some suck that needs to be embraced. The first step is not to sugar coat it, but to call it what it is.

What suck do you need to embrace?

Back when eight characters were enough and caps didn't matter, my first password was "john1010." Special characters weren't allowed, let alone required. I know because when I tried John10:10. Jesus embraced the suck when he said,

The thief comes only to steal, kill, & destroy. I have come that they may have life, & have it more abundantly.

-Jesus

Living *tov* means embracing full life. Scientists can tell you the half-life of everything from plutonium (24,100 years for Pu-239) to Prozac (4-6 days). Half-life is how long it takes until potency is at half of what it was originally. Living *tov* isn't about half-life but abundant life. So let's get living!

253

MOVEMENT VII
SUCCESSION

idea ONE:
SABBATICAL

With the help of a sizable grant, I'd planned the most epic Sabbatical ever. After four years as Youth Director, three as a Postmodern Missionary, three as Executive Director of Educational Development, and ten as Sr. Pastor, Promise said I was long overdue for a Sabbatical.

It would have came two years earlier, but my appendix almost exploded, so I missed the grant deadline the first year, anesthesia and grant writing don't mix well. The next year the grant application was rejected, but as they say, "third times a charm."

Our first month was England. Tricia has always loved great literature, so we were spending a few days at the Bronte Sisters Parsonage, then a few more at Jane Austen's house. It wasn't just the classics, we'd scheduled some time at Highclere Castle (Downton Abbey) and J.K. Rowling's studio.

Cambridge was our next stop, not just for a visit. My doctoral program had three advances (because why retreat when you could advance), one was on the campus of Cambridge.

After that, we'd rented a loft above a pub in the West End for a week of theater. Our tickets were amazing: third row, center to *Cursed Child*,[142] front row to *Hamilton*[143] (which I'm very curious how it plays in England), and an insider scoop for day-of seats to more shows.

Tricia would fly back home, and I'd spend six weeks walking across Spain. Ernest Hemingway wrote about *The Camino de Santiago* in *The Sun Also Rises*,[144] so I'd booked a table in Paris where he and Fitzgerald first met. The train stoped in Bordeaux, so I lined up a wine tasting... Bordeaux in Bordeaux.

Walking *the Camino* was intended to be a time to look back on 25 years of professional church work (I'd served 5 years outside of Promise), and to look forward, asking God to shed some light on what the next 25 might hold. Although I'd walk four days, from St. Jean to Pamplona (stopping at hotel Hemingway stayed at and wrote about) the deep reflection and prayer wouldn't start until after a few days at San Fermín Festival (aka the Running of the Bulls). The Chair of our Board and my wife made me write into the grant balcony rental as a promise to watch and not run.

Alexander Shai[145] suggests time for reentry, even that was built in. Sabbatical would conclude with Tricia, Kaitlyn, Adeline, and myself, spending two weeks at Disney. We'd booked hotels: the Grand Floridian, a suite on the Boardwalk to share with friends, and the Wilderness Lodge. We even ended with a reservation at Victoria and Albert's Chefs table. Adeline couldn't eat, but at the time she could see and smell the experience.

If you were writing a grant for a four month Sabbatical (so money really isn't a hurdle), how would you spend four months?

The guiding question for the grant was, "What makes your heart sing?"

Week One _____
_____
_____
_____
_____

Week Two _____
_____
_____
_____
_____

Week Three _____
_____
_____
_____
_____

Week Four _____
_____
_____
_____
_____... that's only the first month

Week Five _____
_____
_____
_____
_____

Week Six_____
_____
_____
_____
_____

Week Seven_____
_____
_____
_____
_____

Week Eight _____
_____
_____
_____
_____... eight weeks, make month two

Week Nine_____
_____
_____
_____

Week Ten_____
_____
_____
_____

Week Eleven_____
_____
_____
_____

Week Twelve_____
_____
_____
_____... all those fifth days of the month add up,

we have an extra week...Week Thirteen _____
_____
_____
_____
_____
_____

... and the fourth month starts with
Week Fourteen_____
_____
_____
_____
_____

Week Fifteen_____
_____
_____
_____
_____

Week Sixteen_____
_____
_____
_____
_____

Week Seventeen_____
_____
_____
_____
_____

The lions share of my plan, a six week walk,
was the Camino. Pilgrims on the *Camino* carry
credential to prove they walked. Along the
way, at hostels (called *albergue*), churches, and
pubs stamp it. Santiago, where James started

a church, is the destination. Along with visiting Hemingway and Fitzgerald sites, getting my first stamp at St. James tower was the plan. I'd walk along the Seine, 90 minutes to Notre Dame to get my second stamp.

April 15, 2019, Notre Dame caught fire. My grant application had just been turned in, so I was amending my plans before it was even approved. Maybe this was a hint of things to come. Everything you read was scheduled for the Summer of 2020.

Clarity for the next chapter of my life, which I'd hoped to get on a six week walk, came on a three day hike. With Spain, and the rest of the world closed, because of Covid. I tried to pivot. Throwing a hammock in my pack, I'd hike the Kentucky Bourbon trail.

I hadn't expected all the single pump gas stations and mom and pop shops, where I'd fill my water, to be closed because of Covid. Three days in Kentucky heat without water landed me in a hospital, pretty close to death. It also had what Seth Jones informed me was an ESE (Extraordinary Spiritual Experience).

What you are reading (and the coaching that accompanies) was my next step in life. The clarity I was seeking was abundant.

Just as Sabbath should happen every seventh day, Sabbatical should happen every seventh year. I wrote

Having kissed death, my energy levels were low for months. I had time to ponder. Viewing life through a 6:1 lens put some things in perspective. On my third Sabbatical, I'd have to start taking Social Security. By my fourth Sabbatical I'd be well into retirement age.

Dreaming about what to do on Sabbatical was lots of fun, but asking, "What has to happen in the next six years, so the organization doesn't need me for the seventh?" became essential.

Looking back to the creation poem in Genesis, I noticed the first couple days were forming, so just to get the ball rolling what structures do you have to have in place in the first two years or so?

Year One: (20____-20____)

Year Two (20____-20____)

Year Three (20____-20____)

Part way through the third day, things transition from forming to filling. The fourth day stars filling the second day sky, and overflowing as the source of the day, one light. Fifth day fowl, fill second day sky and the fish overflow to sixth day sea. Sixth day people and animals, fill third day land.

We are much better off when we form before we fill, but often we need to think about how something is going to be filled before we form it.

It's a muddle; sometimes, it's helpful to think of the filling first.

We shape our buildings; thereafter they shape us.
- Sir Winston Churchill

Year Three (20____-20____)

Usually, the transition from forming to filling happens in the midst of the third year, so it's listed twice — both in forming and filling.

Year Four (20____-20____)

Year Five (20____–20____)

Year Six (20____–20____).

idea TWO
ASK

Sometimes, the best way to make a point is a sports analogy. I'm not a sports guy. I watch the Super Bowl for the commercials, every semiotician does.

Movies about sports are a different story. From Rocky and Rudy to Space Jam and Moneyball, I'm 100% a sports movie guy.

When Scott was a Pastoral Intern he picked up on this. He's not just a Packer's fan, he's an owner. Scott has the framed certificate to prove it. For Christmas, Scott got me a picture of Jordan, Pippen, and Rodman — the stars of the '93 Chicago Bulls. Other than the Broncos, when we lived outside Denver and John Elway was quarterback, Da Bulls were the only team I knew anything about.

I'm not overstating this, in our house, my daughters call it all (basketball, football, baseball) "sports ball." As a semiotician, not a sports guy, I know that one position in football has changed the meaning of a word: receiver.

Linguistically, there used to be a difference between accept and receive. Accept was active. You have to do something to accept.

Receive was passive, the receiver didn't do anything. That's not the case with receivers in football. Greats, like Jerry Rice (see what I did there Scott), are anything but passive.

Realizing and remembering just how much we've
passively received should lead us to be thankful.
What have you truly received today? What are
your unearned, unmerited, undeserved, free gifts?

Today, mine was Hank remembered my name. He's
a new Barista at my Starbucks, who transferred
from another store. Sure, I paid for my Tall Pike
and the fact we share a name had something to
do with it, but still, he remembered and called
me by name. That was a gift.

When we make it a habit, to recall what we've received, we start to realize how much is a gift. Maybe you don't see anything today, that's OK... look back.

What have you received in the past year, or decade?

It's not that happy people are thankful, its thankful people are happy.

More than happiness, remembering what we've received changes the way active participation is viewed. I never asked my parents to make love. I didn't pour the wine or light the candles, but I was conceived. My life started passively, from that point on active participation is stewardship, but my life started passively.

Succession is stewardship. Sabbatical, done well, leads to succession. Action will have to happen, but freely receiving (rather than rejecting) changes the game.

Irwin Mallin studied law at Syracuse, practiced in New York, then got bored, so he picked up a PhD and started teaching. When he entered the classroom, he pulled a chair next to the desk and sat down, at our level. Irwin told the class to move desks into a circle, so we could see each other. Every class started with a question of the day, from "What sucks?" to "What's your favorite movie?"

When he found out I was dyslexic, he initiated a meeting with me, talked through my paper to help me organize thoughts, then connected me with an editor. After one semester, he encouraged me to go to grad school, saying, "If you teach, I call dibs on being your mentor."

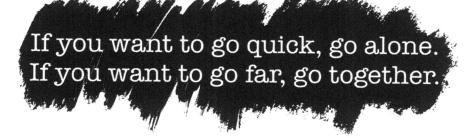

If you want to go quick, go alone.
If you want to go far, go together.

Professors hate education being seen as a commodity. If it's a commodity, they are a cog. At the same time, many embrace being "the sage on a stage." A big jug / little mug model makes whatever's in the big jug a commodity. Irwin rejected little mugs, believing every student had a gift they were trying to give. He didn't commodify education and he didn't reject gifts. In that, Irwin built community.

Think though your organization. What are the
commodities?

What are gifts people want to give?

Which gifts are received, which are rejected and
why?

Where is the community?

Healthy, vibrant, life-giving things happen in community. Toxic, unjust, evil things sometimes happen there too. If you are thinking: "community good commodity bad," first, own that caveman speak is pretty amazing, but stop anyway.

Coffee is a commodity, plain and simple. I'm not attempting to give financial advice, but you could invest in coffee futures.

I've been a coffee guy for a while. Every morning, Tricia and I make a pot. On special occasions, I'll use a French Press, V60 pour over, or an Aeropress, we've collected coffee tools and coffee toys. When Chris came over all the toys were on the table. He owns Muletown Coffee and I figured he'd want a Chemex, the toy I didn't have.

Muletown roasts some amazing beans (go to www.MuletownCoffee.com — they ship), but Chris wasn't caught up on tools and toys. He has realized the value of coffee is not as a commodity, but utilizing the commodity for community. "Coffee is an excuse," he said, "for this," gesturing to me and him at the table talking until the pot ran dry.

271

Community is relational capital (page 50) and is more valuable than commodity (financial capital, page 47). How can you use commodity to build community?

I have coffee with a lot of nones and dones. They are the fastest growing religious group in America today. A done said,

Churches care more about market share, than gospel share(ing).

Leveraging commodity for community is a great trade, but it doesn't well work the other way. Where are you commodifying something that should be community?

To get really practical, learning to ask might be the best way to build community.

In Full disclosure, I viewed coaching as a commodity. When I was challenged to make it more accessible, we embraced a pay it forward model — building community.

To get started, I'd have to ask people for help. Specifically, I'd have to ask people for money. This felt scary and icky, practicing what you preach is hard.

146

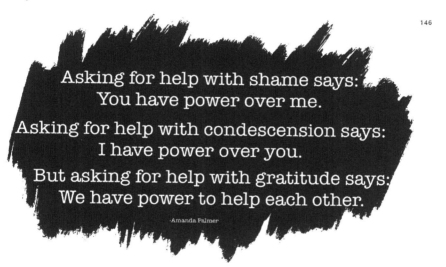

Asking for help with shame says: You have power over me.

Asking for help with condescension says: I have power over you.

But asking for help with gratitude says: We have power to help each other.

-Amanda Palmer

What do you need to ask for?

Who do you need to ask?

Succession, is all about asking.

Take your time with this. Before Jesus asked
people to be his disciples, he thought it through
for 40 days. He prayed and fasted, and was
tempted. Sometimes who we ask for what is the
most important decision we make.

idea THREE:
CAPACITY

When I became Pastor and the congregation jumped from a weekly attendance of about 120, to over 300 within my first few months. It was *tov*...maybe. We added a second service, then attempted (and failed) to add a third. What a year!

The regional leadership of our denomination saw what was going on with our attendance and had me fill out a survey about church growth. My ego wanted to answer that it was because of me.

Where people came from, told the real story.

Our "growth" was merely gaining market share Almost 100% people from other congregations. The churches people were coming from weren't just Christian, but Lutheran, and from the LC–MS (the same sub-set of the same denomination).

Social spaces were leaving one public space and coming to to another, but I got the credit.

If you've experienced organizational "growth" it's essential to ask how much is really a social space shift? Whether to call shifts growth is a discussion worth having. If you are a "growing" organization (church or otherwise) it starts by asking, "Where is that growth coming from?"

I gave you room becasue this might be one of the most important questions to talk about with your team.

Years later (and yes, I mentioned this in the last idea), I heard

Churches care more about market share, than gospel share(ing).

I couldn't argue. The woman said it as part of the reason she left organized religion.

That conversation is why, to be a *Brother Dog* Congregation, you agree to work with us to ensuring at least 6-8 other congregations from 2-3 other denominations are at the One Day Event. We want to share, not capture market share or be part of social spaces shifts.

Brother Dog could team up with half a dozen churches out of the gate. When we crunched the numbers, every One Day event would add 2-3 other organizations. If we started with 4, the next year we would have at least 8 (12, if each event added 3 organizations). Since we were starting at Back-to-School time (August / September) and One Day events would happen on Saturdays, my event capacity would be maxed in year two — there are only so many dates on the calendar.

Even if we figured out a way to add more One Day events, 8 would turn to 16 in year 3, and that's adding two grousp. If we did add 3, rather than 12 we'd be at 36. Could I spend 36 hours a week coaching and still get everything else I need to get done, done?

The answer is no!

Lunch is a great time for coaching. Since, I'm traveling Friday and Monday to get to the One Day, I've got 3 days to coach (Tuesday, Wednesday, and Thursday).

This is how I found my capacity:

6:30	Meds
7:00	Coffee with Tricia
8:00	New Content
COACHING	
10:30	1:30 Eastern
11:45	11:45 Central
1:00	12:00(N) Mountain
2:15	12:15 Pacific
3:30	Gym
5:00	Emails
6:00	Done

I can do "business stuff" while traveling, but my coaching capacity is 12 at a time.

Thankfully, overworking as a Youth Director in Dallas, then having a church "grow" quickly my first year as a pastor, taught me to pay attention to my capacity. If your *tov*, whatever it is, took off (and it will) what would your capacity be?

Sabbatical forces us to think about structure, capacity calls us to think of succession. I wanted to help 100 churches find and live their *miyn tov* before I went on Sabbatical, but to get there we planned to prune. Rather than start with 4, we'd start with 2.

80/20

If you've done fundraising you've heard of the Pareto Principle (aka the 80/20 rule). Long before I learned it, I ordered pizza for a Junior High lock-in, and saw it in action.

Cici's, a pizza place across the street had a "youth group special." Order five one topping pizzas for $5 each, and they threw in a sixth for free. I could feed the whole group for $50.

One night Jake and his friends didn't show up and we had 11 pizza's left. It turned out the other 20 kids (80%) ate about a slice each. Eight slices in a pie means I could feed them three pizzas. Jake and his four friends (80%) were eating two pizzas each!

Time after time 80% of your volunteers will do 20% of the work, and 20% will do 80% of it. When it comes to donations 20% of your givers will give 80% of the budget (and 80% will give 20%). Even in pizza, there will always be Jake and his friends.

Where have you seen the Pareto principle play out?

If you work five days a week, each day is about 20%. That means one day of work gets you 80% of your results. The rest of each week, only get you 20%. Another way to look at it is in an 8 hour work day, a little more than an hour and a half, gets you 80% of your results.

What are the things you spend 20% of your time on that get you 80% of your results?

For me this was coaching, so I upped it to four hours a day, three days a week. New content was another big one for me, so it gets 90 minutes every day.

What are the things you spend 80% of your time on that only get you 20% of your results?

For me it's emails, so I will not spend more than an hour doing them. My auto reply tells people this and explains why.

By my math, if we doubled down, and rather than spending 20% of our time doing the things that get 80% of the results, we spend 40% of our time doing those things, we'd get 160% of the results.

Maybe we'll have to spend another 20% doing things that don't produce much, but can you imagine 60% more results than you are getting now and 3 day work weeks (or being done by lunch everyday)!

In a letter to Corinth, what Paul writes gets translated, "imitate me."[147] What he had done is taken the time to figure out how he did what he did and provide the churches with a template. It wasn't about the Church in Corinth imitating Paul, they were still *miyn* (that means "of its kind"). He was giving them a template.

Dedicating time to developing a template early on, in the forming days, multiplies capacity. In my schedule, this is "new content." It is one of those things that will give you 80% of your results because you can share it.

What do you have that people can "imitate?"

idea FOUR
40/70 FAITH

With two ideas left in the book, I have a
confession. Movies taught me about authors.
I bought some tweed jackets at a Thrift shop,
the ones with elbow patches and picked up a
pipe. Since I have asthma, I couldn't smoke the
pipe, but I lit it and carried it around the local
watering hole for artists and academics.

The problem is, back then, I didn't write; at least
not regularly. It's not the gin gimlet, the pipe,
or the tweed jacket, but showing up at the page
every day and writing. If you don't write you
aren't a writer, plain and simple. You may play
the part of an author, but you aren't a writer.

I blame Thoreau.

> I went to the woods because I wished
> to live deliberately, to front only the
> essential facts of life, and see if I could
> not learn what it had to teach, and not,
> when I came to die, discover that I had
> not lived. I did not wish to live what was
> not life, living is so dear; nor did I wish
> to practice resignation, unless it was
> quite necessary. I wanted to live deep
> and suck out all the marrow of life, to
> live so sturdily and Spartan-like as to
> put to rout all that was not life, to cut a
> broad swath and shave close, to drive life
> into a corner, and reduce it to its lowest
> terms...[148]

is misleading at best. His buddy, Ralph Waldo
Emerson, owned the land on Walden and let
him build and write there. How "sturdy and

spartan like" is borrowing a buddy's land? He could walk to town and did so every day or two. Mrs. Thoreau (his mom) had him over for Sunday dinner and sent him home with a basket of food, like many moms do. People read Walden and get a very different picture of being an author. At least Henry David Thoreau wrote.

Unfortunately, this isn't just an author, or artist thing. When people find, and attempt to live *tov* a bit of fantasy takes over. Religious folk mix this with faith, and it can get down right dangerous. (There is a reason we started with spaghetti numbers).

Colin Powell, former Chairman of the joint chief of staff, had a 40-70 rule for making decisions. He didn't say it, but that's where faith lives.

To avoid making bad decisions, you need at least 40% of the information according to Colin Powell. Watch a movie about authors, read some books like Walden, and you have 10%, maybe 15% of the information on what it takes to be an author. Still some people will attempt to act on that little information. Some people call acting on no information faith, it's not faith its foolishness.

Be honest, where do you need to get a little more information before you act?

I'm amazed how many Bible Studies and Sermons are preached at 30% information. Did you ever notice when Peter and John argue with the priest, they end up in prison. When Jesus argues with them, he's fine (at least for a while). In fact, when Jesus throws a temple tantrum and flips the tables of money changers, the temple guards don't arrest him.

Attributing this to Jesus' divinity, or "God's will" falls in that foolish category. It's much better to admit you are at 15%, and say, "I don't know."

Let's move the needle and see if we can get, from foolishness to faith.

Jewish kids in Jesus' day officially started school at 5 or 6 years old. They called it Bet Sefer (House of the Book) and they would attempt to memorize the Genesis though Malachi. The goal was to know what the teacher, called a Rabbi, knew.

Most turned 13, went and learned the family trade, but around 12 years old some were siphoned off for Bet Midrash (House of Question) with the hopes of becoming an actual disciple (sometimes called a talmudin). A disciple didn't just know what the Rabbi knew, they did what the Rabbi did.

Today Ivy League Schools are the best of the best. Geograohically, they are spread around. In Jesus' day, all the best Rabbi's were in Jerusalem. Jesus' parents took him to Jerusalem for a festival when he was 12 and he interviewed for Bet Talmud. That's what "sitting amoung the Rabbi's listening to them and asking them questions" means. He was interviewing.

Rabbi's like Universities aren't foolish. They knew enough about a potential disciple that they had faith the disciple could make it. A guy like me had a 40% shot of making it, so I got into Ball State on academic probation. For Jesus,

"Everyone who heard him," included the leading Rabbis, and the fact they "were amazed at his understanding and answers"[149] means he not only got in, but he was more than 70% – honors college material.

People wonder what Jesus did between 13 and 30. The Bible doesn't tell us because it doesn't have to. Today, if an 18 year old interviewed at Harvard and Harvard was impressed by her interview, everybody knows what she'd be doing for the next 4 years.

Like Ivy League schools today, it was expensive to study in Jerusalem and Jesus was from a working class home. If only he had something he could cash in and pay for school. Maybe, gold he'd gotten as a birthday present from some wiseguy would cover the cost.

My guess is he had more in common with the working class temple guards than the trust fund kids he was in class with. He learned their names and was kind to them. Sometimes, when you know the cops you get away with stuff.

I'm not claiming this as fact, but my guess is this reading gets beyond foolishness and to the 40% mark where we can exercise faith.

foolish   FAITH

0%.   40%   70%   100%

As an individual, or orginization what are areas
you think are *miyn tov*, but you know you are not
at 40% yet?

What needs to happen to get beyond 40%?

Some get excited about finding their *tov* and want to jump into it headlong. One corporate graphic designer, was two clicks from *tov*, quit his job to design skate boards. Within the year he designed the *tov* and *Ra* boards for me, and a deck for Tony Hawk.

That is less than 40% of the story. Over years, He also built up enough client work, so that he knew he could financially support himself. Beside that, squirreled away a full year cushion and told himself if it got below a certain point he'd go back to corporate life.

If you are going to take that leap of faith, and quit a job, never do it with less than 6 months cash in hand. You really should have a year. It's going to take time to get traction. Things won't go as you planned and if you get down to the window of three months left, you'll probably want to start applying for job like the one you quit.

Getting to 40% moves from foolishness to faith, but getting beyond 70% moves from faith to fact.

In school, 70% is a **C**, and **C** means average. 65% of Americans believe they are above average (just let that sink in for a second), so a **C** is seen as low. Statistics have shown that a little less than 16% of people are actually above average.

We rarely have above average information. Colin Powell knew if he waited until he had 70% of the information, it would be too late, and the decision would be made for you. I'd argue 70% is where we move from faith to fact.

There is nothing wrong with fact, it's just not faith. Where could you be excercising faith, but you are waiting for fact?

Don't wait until you have 71% to make a decision, it is too late. At 71%, the decision has been made for you and you are reacting. To live *tov* means to live in 40-70 faith.

You don't have to change jobs to live your *tov*, maybe it's just a tweak or two. However, if success is succession, you will need to exercise some faith. This becomes central as you decide who to disciple.

FISHERMEN, TAXMAN INSURRECTIONIST

Find your *tov*.

See it,   Say it.   Separate it...
divide it and let it dance, and then you die. If
your *tov* dies with you, can it be called success?

I think I mentioned.

Succession is success.

but it's also an act of faith.

Remember,

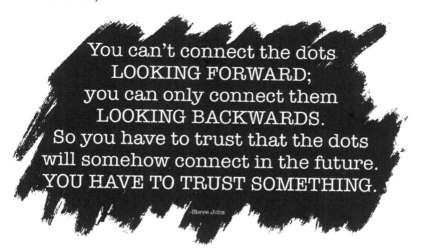

You can't connect the dots
LOOKING FORWARD;
you can only connect them
LOOKING BACKWARDS.
So you have to trust that the dots
will somehow connect in the future.
YOU HAVE TO TRUST SOMETHING.

-Steve Jobs

The success of Jesus' succession isn't hard to see, but remember Judas and Peter both betrayed him. If you are going to get serious about succession, be ready for both success and betrayal.

By this point, you know your *tov* and are ready to help others find and live theirs. Who is on your team that you are helping find *tov*?

Mike Breen has dedicated his life to discipleship, and developed the square as a model to explain what happens. When someone is asked into a discipling relationship, Breen points out they have high enthusiasm and high confidence, but low experience and low competency. In all reality, they don't know what they don't know. As one who is summoned to lead, at this stage, it's best to give high direction, high example, low consensus, low explanation.[150]

How are you inviting people into succession?

The way Jesus did this, was simply saying, "Come, follow me. I will make you fishers of men."[151] At least that's how he invited Simon, Andrew, James, and John.

We only know what six of Jesus' twelve disciples did. Those four were fisherman, hardworking blue collar folk. They had prime sea side real estate, but were taxed.

Historians debate on the amount of tax. We know Rome took a cut and so did the temple. Even if there were an honest tax collector, "Don't kill the messenger," is a phrase for a reason. I haven't met many who love the IRS nowadays. Some things never change. So Jesus put an agent named Levi (aka Matthew) on his team. Homogenization was not the goal, succession was.

Iron sharpens iron,[152] but no one gets sharp without a clash between the two. If the tension between the working class small business owner and the IRS wasn't enough, and to have multiple people with the same name, Jesus recruited another Simon, an insurrectionist. We don't know what kind of Zealot he was, but one group (the Sicarii) was named after the dagger they stabbed Romans and Roman sympathizers with. The phrase cloak and dagger started with them, so the vibe has some staying power. Still, Jesus asked him to be on the team.

Remember, Jesus' instructions were to start making disciples in Jerusalem. This is where they were, where people were like them. Don't drop the were and read that as where people like them. Having a shared culture is essential starting place. Liking each other isn't.

Who is in your orbit (not your immediate team), that you might want to help find *tov*?

As you look at those on your list, are they all fisherman? Who is the IRS agent? Is an insurrectionist in your immediate community?

Don't be foolish, know at least 40% about these people. It may take more than a cup of coffee. At the same time, you will never get beyond 70%. Don't wait for fact, succession deals with people, so we've got to operate in faith.

You've got to see, before you say. Envision inviting them to find and live *tov* with you.

Before we started Brother Dog, the decision was made to require churches to invite 6-8 leadership teams (only 2-3 people each) from at least 2-3 other denominations. It was a baby step, what's yours?

You are well beyond 40%, my guess is that you might be pushing 60% or 70%. It's time to act.

WARNING: They will fall off the cliff. Mike points out the second stage of discipleship (D2) is unenthusiasticly incompetent, epitomized by: low enthusiasm, low confidence, low experience, low competence. He draws the square like this

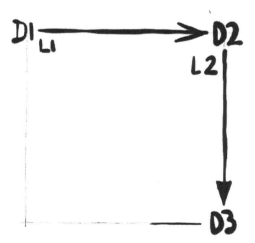

Offer high direction, high discussion, high example, high accessibility, and they will find and live *tov*, like you did.

You aren't going out alone, if there is anything I can do to help, please ask.

BOOKLIST

Early 1996, around my 21st birthday, I was in a greenroom somewhere in California. Years later, I'd become a youth director, attend conferences, and realize Mike Yaconelli was the stuff of legendary. That day, he was another event speaker I'd never heard of, but he took time to invest in me, a confused kid with an olive drab deathlock hair-do.

We probably only interacted for 20 minutes. More than a lifetime later, his words echo. Topping my take-aways, "Whenever you can, ask for a book list."

Getting booklists has paid dividends.

Some of the books in the endnotes, are mere citations. Others, are definately worth the read. These are 22, mentioned somewhere in this book, that should be on your shelf. Be warned, they'll only be there for a moment. More often then not, you'll loan them out. Friends will be reading them, mark them up, and "forget" to return them. That's the problem with a great booklist.

Breen, Mike. *Building a Discipleship Culture* (3rd Edition). Pawley Island: 3DM. 2017.

Brewin, Kester. 2012. *Mutiny!: Why We Love Pirates and How They Can Save Us.* London: Vaux.

•Brown, Brené. *Daring Greatly: How the Courage to Be Vulnerable Transforms the Way We Live, Love, Parent and Lead.* New York: Avery. 2012.

Brown, Sunni. *The Doodle Revolution: Unlock the Power to Think Differently.* Westminster, London: Portfolio, 2015.

Cameron, Julia. *The Artist's Way: A Spiritual Path to Higher Creativity.* New York: Tarcher / Penguin, 1992.

Collins, Jim. *Good to Great: Why Some Companies Make the Leap...and Others Don't.* New York: HarperCollins. 2001.

Edwards, Betty. *Drawing on the Right Side of the Brain.* New York: Tarcher Perigee, 2012.

Gilbert, Elizabeth. *Big Magic: Creative Living Beyond Fear.* New York: Riverhead Books. 2015.

•Gladwell, Malcolm. *The Tipping Point: How Little Things Can Make a Big Difference.* New York: Back Bay Books. 2002.

•Gladwell, Malcolm. *Outliers: The Story of Success.* New York: Little, Brown and Company. 2008.

•Goff, Bob. *Love Does: Discover A Secretly Incredible Life In An Ordinary World.* Nashville: Thomas Nelson. 2012.

MacKenzie, Gordon. *Orbiting the Giant Hairball: A Corporate Fool's Guide to Surviving with Grace.* New York: Viking. 1996.

McChesney, Chris, Sean Covey, and Jim Huling. *The 4 Disciplines of Execution.* New York: Free Press. 2016.

•Miller, Donald. *A Million Miles in a Thousand Years: What I Learned While Editing My Life.* Nashville: Thomas. 2009.

Palmer, Amanda. *The Art of Asking: How I Learned to Stop Worrying and Let People Help.* New York: Grand Central Publishing. 2014.

Shenk, Joshua. *Powers of Two: Finding the Essence of Innovation in Creative Pairs.* New York: Houghton Mifflin Harcourt. 2014.

Silvers, Derek. 2015. *Anything You Want: 40 Lessons for a New Kind of Entrepreneur.* New York: Portfolio. 2015.

•Sweet, Leonard. *Summoned to Lead.* Grand Rapids: Zondervan. 2004.

Tierney, John and Roy Baumeister. *The Power of Bad: How the Negitivity Effect Rules Us and How We Can Rule It.* New York: Penguin Press. 2019.

Wilson, C. McNair. *Hatch! Brainstorming Secrets of a Theme Park Designer.* Colorado Springs: Book Villages. 2012.

•Yaconelli, Mike. *Dangerous Wonder: The Adventure of Childlike Faith.* Colorado Springs: Navpress. 1998.

Z, Jay. *Decoded.* New York: Random House. 2010.

A fuller, ever expanding, and almost never up to date list is at www.FindYourTov.com/booklist

Every now and again, I mark an author with an asterisk. This means I try and read everything they publish, and have yet to be disappointed. I can't recommend books by Brené Brown, Donald Miller, or Mike Yaconelli enough. In addition to books, the podcasts of Malcolm Gladwell (*Revisionist History*) and Bob Goff (*Dream Big*) are worth a listen.

Leonard Sweet is in a league of his own. When I googled his name and the word book, 51 images of books he's authored appeared. I haven't read them all. However, I had the honor of learning from him in the Doctor of Ministry in Semiotics, Church, and Culture Program at George Fox Universtiy / Portland Seminary. I could not recommend his work or this program more highly. Learn more at www.georgefox.edu/seminary/programs/dmin-semiotics/index.html

ENDNOTES

MOVEMENT I: ORIGIN STORY
1 *The Power of Bad* by John Tierney & Roy Baumeister
2 *Good to Great* by Jim Collins
3 *Powers of Two* by Joshua Shenkt
4 *Big Magic* by Elizabeth Gilbert
5 *Daring Greatly* by Brené Brown

MOVEMENT II: SUCCESS
6 Brown, Brené. *The Gifts of Imperfection: Let Go of Who You Think You're Supposed to Be and Embrace Who You Are.* Center City: Hazelden. 2010.
7 Griffo, Ilana. *Mind Your Business: A Workbook to Grow Your Creative Passion Into a Full-time Gig.* Bend: Blue Star Press. 2019.
8 Blue House Fitness (www.bluehousefitness.com)
9 Just Capital Quotient (www.JustCapitalQuotient.com)
10 Phelps, Michael. *Beneath the Surface: My Story.* New York: Sports Publishing. 2016.
11 *Love Does* by Bob Goff
12 Rundman, Jonathan. "German Flag (2009)." Placeless Songs, Salt Lady Records, 2016. https://jonathanrundman.bandcamp.com/track/german-flag-2009
13 The Notorious B.I.G (featuring Mase and Sean Combs) "Mo Money Mo Problems." Life After Death, Bad Boy Entertainment, 1997.
14 *Outliers by* Malcom Gladwell --It's worth noting, Gladwell is citing neurologist Daniel Levitin here.
15 I translate Matthew 28:18-20 "As you are going, make disciples (with this two step template): (1) baptizing them in the name of the Father, and the Son, and the Holy Spirit, and (2) teaching them to obey everything I have commanded you.
Invitation and Challenge are the two step process of disciple making. Sharing identity (baptism in the name of) is the highest invitation one can offer. Likewise, a command to "obey everything taught" is the highest challenge. I lifted "Invitation and Challenge" language from *Building a Discipleship Culture* by Mike Breen.
16 Dr. Dave Switzer was head of the Communication Department at IPFW (Indiana University - Purdue University, Fort Wayne) and a baseball umpire — the two formed a beautiful mandorla. He introduced me to a proper Martini, and coined "Necessary not sufficient," one of his many perfectly distilled lines.
17 Matthew tells about Jesus baptism in chapter 3, particularly 3:13-17. His temptation was at the end of his Sabbatical fast and is recorded in 4:1-11.
Matthew 4:12-17 includes him hearing about John being put in prison, leaving Nazareth and moving to Galilee. It is likely the sermon in Nazareth Luke recorded (4:14-30).

Since preaching in the synagogue happened Saturday, and he left preaching to heal Simon Peter's mother-in-law (Luke 4:38), it is most likely that Matthew 4:18-22 happened before Jesus had preached a second sermon.

18 Mark 6:7-13
19 Luke 9:1-6
20 Luke 10:1-23
21 I heard this at a confrence and I know Rabbi Allen said it. However, I can't track him down or remember the confrence.
22 I Corinthians 15:6
23 *Anything You Want by* Derek Silvers

Movement III: SEE

24 In an Observer article, Kenneth Tynan described a 1966 Cannes Film Festival's conversation between Clouzot and Godard Quote Investigator. "Films Should Have a Begining, a Middle, and an End." January 4, 2020, https://quoteinvestigator.com/2020/01/04/middle/#note-437219-1 adds greater context and history.
25 Hoffmann, Yoel. *Japanese Death Poems: Written by Zen Monks and Haiku Poets on the Verge of Death.* Rutland/Tokyo: Charles E. Tuttle Company. 1986. (p.190).
26 Shakespeare, William. 1609. Sonnet 18. 1609.
27 *Building a Discipleship Culture* by Mike Breen
28 *Drawing on the Right Side of the Brain* by Betty Edwards
29 *Orbiting the Giant Hairball* by Gordon MacKenzie
30 Matthew 13:13 ESV
31 *The Doodle Revolution* by Suni Brown
Gray, David, Sunni Brown, and James Macanufo. *Gamestorming: A Playbook for Innovators, Rulebreakers, and Changemakers.* Sebastopol: O'Reilly. 2010.
32 Night is Electric "Start a War" Outside My Head, https://www.nightiselectric.com, 2018.
33 In 1907, Sir Earnest Shackleton personally ordered 25 cases of Mackinlay's Rare Old Highland Malt Whisky for his team, Nimrod. In 2007, three cases were found frozen at the Cape Royds base camp. Shortly thereafter, Mackinlay put out this tribute based on the found bottles.
34 *Summoned to Lead* by Leonard Sweet
35 I Samuel 3
36 Lakoff, George and Mark Johnson. *Metaphors We Live By.* Chicago: The University of Chicago Press. 1980. Title of Chapter 3, pp. 10-13 unpack this, for example "metaphorical structuring involved here is partial, not total. If it were total, one concept would actually *be* the other, not merely understood in terms of it." (p. 13) Understood this way, metaphor is kin to what I Corinthians 13:12 is unpacking. "For now we see in a mirror dimly, but then face to face. Now I know in part, then I shall know fully, even as I have been fully known." Notably, this is immediatly preceded by, "When I was a child, I spoke as a child, I thought like a child, I reasoned like a child. When I became a man, I gave up childish ways."

37 *Drawing on the Right Side of the Brain by* Betty Edwards
38 The Beach Boys "Good Vibrations." Good Vibrations, Capitol, 1966.
39 Find Lauren's work on instagram @JuneGarden or https://ldavis0988.wixsite.com/wordsinthegarden
40 Find Sophia's work on instagram or twitter @sopheulm
41 Bouchard, R. Philip. "The 5 Senses, or Maybe 7, Probably 9, Perhaps 11." Medium, November 8, 2016: https://medium.com/the-philipendium/the-5-senses-or-maybe-7-probably-9-perhaps-11-f9e6c54f76f0
42 *Hatch! by* C. McNair Wilson
43 Albee, Edward. The Zoo Story. 1958.

Movement IV: Sabbath

44 Cash, Johnny "Thirteen." American Recodings
45 Danzing "Thirteen." 6:66 Satans Child, Evilive/E-Magine, 1999.
46 Genesis 1:1 is a verse of 7 words, the next verse is 14 (7x2), this underscores *tov* (multiplication) as the central theme of this poem, Genesis, and the entire Bible.
47 Stanley Kubrick, director. *The Shining*. Burbank: Warner Brothers, 1980. --Prior credit as a James Howell Proverb in English, Italian, French, and Spanish 1659.
48 I saw this on a homemade sign at a Fort for Fitness (www.fort4fitness.org) half marathon.
49 Genesis 1:3-5, *tov* shows up in verse 4.
50 Genesis 1:6-8, nothing is called *tov* this day.
51 Genesis 1:9-10, *tov* is mentioned in 1:10.
52 Genesis 1:11-13, *tov* is mentioned in 1:12.
53 Genesis 1:14-19, *tov* is mentioned in 1:18.
54 Genesis 1:20-23, *tov* is mentioned in 1:21.
55 Genesis 1:24-31, *tov* is mentioned 1:25.
56 We unpack this in the coaching, (and I'll probably dedicate an episode of the Find Your *Tov* podcast to it), but this is what "subdue" and "dominion" in Genesis 1:28 are getting at.
57 Genesis 1:31
58 *The Four Disciplines of Execution by* Chris McChesney, Sean Covey, and Jim Hulling. -- They are referring to Wildly Important Goals (WIGs) and differentiate this from the daily whirlwind we have to deal with continually.
59 Rongnlien, Bob. *Experiential Worship: Encountering God with Heart, Soul, Mind, and Strength*. Colorado Springs: Nav Press. 2004.
60 Kleon, Austin. Thursday, March 16, 2017. "Pay Attention To What You Pay Attention To." https://austinkleon.com/2017/03/16/pay-attention-to-what-you-pay-attention-to
61 McAfee, Joel and Gabe McCauley, dir. *Reconnecting Roots* https://www.reconnectingroots.com
62 Slow Watch (www.slow-watches.com/the-brand)
63 Currey, Mason. *Daily Rituals: How Artists Work*. New York: Alfred A. Knopf. 2014.
64 *The Artist's Way by* Julia Cameron, p. 9-10. --She goes on to address blocking, claiming morning pages are "the

primary tool of creative recovery." She also frames blocking as "the censor," reminding "your censors's negative opinions are not the truth."

65 Exodus 20:8-10
66 Genesis 1:14-15
67 Shaia, Alexander. 2018. *Returning From Camino*. Santa Fe: Journey of Quadratos.
68 Leviticus 25:3-4
69 Stagmeister, Stefan. "The Power of Time Off." TEDGlobal 2009. https://www.ted.com/talks/stefan_sagmeister_the_power_of_time_off/transcript?language=en
70 When people were mentioned in this book, either it was previously published, or I personally contacted them. If they were deceased, I did my best to contact the nearest living relative. In the case of my Dad, Mom and siblings, my sister, Amanda, shared a very different meomory of this story. Season 3 of *Revisionist History*, 2 episodes explore memory variations:
Gladwell, Malcom. "A Polite Word for Liar." Produced by Pushkin. *Revisionist History,* May 31 2018. Podcast MP3 audio, 40:02. https://www.pushkin.fm/podcasts/revisionist-history/a-polite-word-for-liar
_____. "Free Brian Williams." Produced by Pushkin. *Revisionist History,* June 6, 2018. Podcast MP3 audio, 39:36. https://www.pushkin.fm/podcasts/revisionist-history/free-brian-williams#play
71 Quote Investigator. "If You Always Do What You've Always Done, You Always Get What You've Always Gotten." April 25, 2016, https://quoteinvestigator.com/2016/04/25/get
72 Not only is this the soul of a foot (get it), it's the "Footsteps" logo. Over 30 years Bob Rongnlien (www.bo brognlien.com) has developed and lead piligramages that follow the footsteps of Jesus through Isreal and Paul through Turkey and Greece. Since my first trip (mentioned on page 230) Bob has discipled me to lead these 14 day piligramages. When I do, we also engage Finding *Tov.* Find out more at www.footsteps-experience.com
73 Oxford Languages / Google
74 Sweet, Leonard. 2014. *The Well-Played Life: Why Pleasing God Doesn't Have to Be Such Hard Work.* Carol Stream: Tyndale Momentum.
75 *Decoded.* by Jay Z
76 Tebelak, John-Michael. Godspell. 1971.
77 *A Million Miles in a Thousand Years* by Donald Miller
78 Larson, Jonathan. Rent. 1996.
79 Jonathan Larson. "Seasons of Love" Rent (Original Broadway Cast Recording), DreamWorks Records, 1996.
80 Taylor Swift "22" Red: Taylor's Version, Republic Records, 2021. --Citation is "Taylor's Version" to draw attention to the *Ra* of the 2013 release and subsequent ownership issues. Like people, music can not be owned. The best treatment of this idea is explored in *Mutiny!* by Kester Brewin. In keeping with the thesis you can get *Mutiny!* at www.medium.com/mutiny-by-kester-brewin

MOVEMENT V: SAY

81 Austin, J.L. *How To Do Things With Words*. Cambridge: Harvard University Press, 1962. 25.

82 Genesis 1:3-5

83 Propaganda. *Terraform: Building a Better World*. New York: Harper One. 2021.

84 *The Power of Bad* by John Tierney & Roy Baumeister, 27

85 _____, 23.

86 5:1 is called the Gottman ratio named after psychologist John Gottman.

87 Williamson, Marianne. 1996. *A Return to Love: Refklections on the Principles of "A Course in Miracles."* New York: Harper One.

88 James 3:3-8

89 Genesis 1:27l

90 Genesis 1:3

91 A double date exposes the mandorla. Each "us" is counted as a single unit. Mitch Hedberg has a great joke about calling corn on the cob corn... "if you pulled off my arm you wouldn't call it Mitch then put it back on and call me Mitch all together."

92 Dunbar, Robin. *How Many Friends Does One Person Need? Dunbar Number and Other Evolutionary Quirks*. Faber & Faber. 2010.

93 Angell, Kate. *Curveball* (Richmond Rogues Book 2). New York: Love Spell (Dorchester). 2007.

94 Taylor Swift and Aaron Dessner "The 1" Folklore, Republic, 2020.

95 Malcom Gladwell often gets credited with 150 being a tipping point because he cites Dunbar and gives an amazing illustration about how Gore Tex utilizes this tipping point. *The Tipping Point* by Malcolm Gladwell.

96 Acts 1:8

97 Night is Electric "Start a War" Outside My Head, https://www.nightiselectric.com, 2018. (Video — *https://youtu.be/-xJN1UzGwJU*

98 Quote Investigator. "No Matter Where You Go, There You Are." November 12, 2020, https://quoteinvestigator.com/2020/11/22/where-you-go

99 Brené Brown: *The Call to Courage*. Directed by Sandra Restrepo. Los Gatos: Netflix, 2019.

100 Genesis 1:28

101 Bob Dylan "Man Gave Names to All the Animals" Slow Train Coming, Columbia, 1979.

102 *Gamestorming* by David Gray, Sunni Brown, and James Macanufo -- SWOT Analysis (p. 212) is one of 40+ "games for exploring" in Chapter Six. Many of these are amazing for getting your team to clarify "what is" and "what can be." Ch7, Games for closing is also helpful is clarifying "what will be" (Movement VI: Separate).

103 Run Hard Rest Well (https://runhardrestwell.org)

104 Before I knew MIke Breen, I asked a question at a workshop and this is what he wrote on the white board.

105 Liberman, Daniel and Michael Long. *The Molecule of More: How a Single Chemical in Your Brain Drives Love, Sex, and Creativity and Will Determine the Fate of the Human Race*. Dallas: BenBella. 2018.

106 Ed Sheeran "Lego House" +, Asylum / Atlantic, 2011.

MOVEMENT VI: **SEPARATE**

107 Good Reads. "Steve Jobs› Quotes› Quoteable Quotes." https://www.goodreads.com/quotes/988332-some-people-say-give-the-customers-what-they-want-but

108 *Hatch! by* C. McNair Wilson, 87–96.

109 _____, 89.

110 _____, 88.

111 _____, 89–90.

112 _____, 90–92.

113 Umoh, Ruth. "The surprising lesson this 25-year-old learned from asking Warren Buffett an embarrassing question." CBS, June 5, 2018. https://www.cnbc.com/2018/06/05/warren-buffetts-answer-to-this-question-taught-alex-banayan-a-lesson.html

114 *The Four Disciplines of Execution* by Chris McChesney, Sean Covey, and Jim Hulling

115 Good Reads. "Michelangelo Buonarrti› Quotes› Quoteable Quotes." https://www.goodreads.com/quotes/1191114-the-sculpture-is-already-complete-within-the-marble-block-before

116 Quote Investigator. "You Just Chip Away Everything That Doesn't Look Like David." June 22, 2014, https://quoteinvestigator.com/2014/06/22/chip-away

117 John 15:3 in the midst of speaking of pruning Jesus says, "You are already clean."

118 ἐгὼ ειμι (Ego Eimi) is an interesting phrase. It is more accurately translated "I, I am" than "I am."

119 John 15:1–3

120 Oxenreider, Tsh. *At Home in the World: Reflections on Belonging While Wandering the Globe*. Nashville: Nelson. 2017.

121 Genesis 1:2–5

122 Genesis 1:9–13

123 *60 minutes*. Season 4, episode 3, "Behind the Scenes with Eminem and Anderson Cooper." Aired October 10, 2010, on CBS.

124 Genesis 1:6–8

125 Original Photo was taken by Eusebius (Guillaume Piolle) and accessed at https://commons.wikimedia.org/wiki File:Chartres_-_portail_royal,_tympan_central.jpg Croping and recoloring was done by A. McKenna

126 John 10:30

127 Matthew 24:36

128 *Orbiting the Giant Hairball* by Gordon MacKenzie, 30.

129 _____, 29.

130 _____, 31.

131 _____, 32.

132 _____, 33.

133 Genius. "Hello,Goodbye." https://genius.com/The-beatles-hello-goodbye-lyrics

134 Quora. "What languages have one word for both 'hello' and 'goodbye'?." accessed Thursday, September 9, 2022. https://www.quora.com/What-languages-have-one-word-for-both-hello-and-goodbye

135 Phelan, Matthew. "The History of 'Hurt People Hurt People'." Slate, September 17, 2019. https://slate.com/culture/2019/09/hurt-people-hurt-people-quote-origin-hustlers-phrase.html

136 Ezekiel 18:20

137 Deuteronomy 5:9

138 Miranda, Lin-Manuel. Hamilton: An American Musical. 2015.

139 *Love Does:*by Bob Goff, 38.

140 *The Art of Asking* by Amanda Palmer

141 Gaiman says, "It's my fault. When I started writing *Coraline*, I wrote my version of the quote in *Tremendous Trifles,* meaning to go back later and find the actual quote, as I didn't own the book, and this was before the Internet. And then ten years went by before I finished the book, and in the meantime I had completely forgotten that the Chesterton quote was mine and not his. I'm perfectly happy for anyone to attribute it to either of us. The sentiment is his, the phrasing is mine." Neil Gaiman on tumblr February 12, 2013 at 12:21AM https://neil-gaiman.tumblr.com/post/42909304300/my-moms-a-librarian-and-planning-to-put-literary

142 Rowling, J. K., Jack Thorne, and John Tiffany. Harry Potter and the Cursed Child. 2016.

143 Miranda, Lin-Manuel. Hamilton: An American Musical. 2015.

144 Hemingway, Ernest. 2006. *The Sun Also Rises.* New York: Scribner.

MOVEMENT VII: SUCCESSION

145 Shaia, Alexander. *Returning from Camino.* Santa Fe: Journey of Quadratos. 2018.

146 *The Art of Asking* by Amanda Palmer

147 I Corinthians 11:1

148 Thoreau, Henry David. 1910. *Walden.* New York: Thomas Y Crowell & Company.

149 Luke 2:47

150 *Building a Discipleship Culture*by Mike Breen

151 Matthew 4:19, Mark 1:17

152 Proverbs 27:17

FIND YOUR TOV
www.FindYourTov.com

If you don't live your *tov*, part of creation is left undone. People can't live *tov*, if they don't know their *tov*. So, we do everything we can to help individuals and orginizations find their *tov*. What you are holding right now, is part of that.

You can use this book by yourself, or with your team. It works alone, but pairs perfectly with coaching. Find out more at www.findyourtov.com

This **SKETCH**book paired with coaching, well to use *tov* language, it bears the most fruit. Because coaching produces results, it keeps getting more expensive. Often this puts it out of reach from individuals and orginizations who would gain the most.

Find Your **TOV** coaching is offered though a 501(c)(3) not for profit company that strives to, among other things, make this coaching accessible. When you donate, every dollar helps people find their *tov*. Find out more, or donate today.

BROTHER DOG
WWW.BROTHERDOG.ONLINE